U.S. Fish & Wildlife Service

# Schoolyard Habitat Project Guide

*A planning guide for creating schoolyard habitat and outdoor classroom projects*

# Schoolyard Habitat Project Guide

*A planning guide for creating schoolyard habitat and outdoor classroom projects*

*Second Edition 2011*

Carolyn Kolstad
U.S. Fish and Wildlife Service
Schoolyard Habitat Program Coordinator
Pacific Southwest Region

Karleen Vollherbst
U.S. Fish and Wildlife Service
Schoolyard Habitat Program Coordinator
Sacramento Fish and Wildlife Office

Karen Kelly Mullin
Principal Consultant
Willow Oak Group, LLC

## Acknowledgements

Many ideas and much inspiration for this national guide were drawn from more than 20 years of dedicated work from biologists in the Chesapeake Bay, Clear Lake Ecological Services and Tulsa Ecological Services field offices. We are also grateful to the many teachers, students, administrators and community members from across the country who have worked tirelessly to create Schoolyard Habitat projects. They have all taken bold steps to connect children with nature.

**Principal contributors:** Britt Eckhardt Slattery, Julie Dieguez, Betty Grizzle, Kathryn Reshetiloff, Flavia Rutkosky

**Special thanks to the following:** Jontie Aldrich, Tekla Ayres, Cheryl Bauer-Armstrong, Renee Brawner, Herb Broda, Jason Cox, Michelle Daubon, Michelle Donlan, Scott Feille, Glenda Franich, Michael Glenn, Rick Hall, Dennis Hartnett, Mark Herzog, Laurie Hewitt, Michelle Hunt, Ron Jones, Akimi King, Carolyn Martus, Rich Mason, Kirk Meyer, Jeri Nolan, Dennis Prichard, Julie Rose, Heather Rydzeski, Barbara Shaughnessy, Tim Smigielski, Julie Study, Elaine Tholen, April Wells, Kacey Wetzel, Susie Wirth, Polly Zimmerman

**Many activities and ideas were provided by the following curricula:**

U.S. Fish and Wildlife Service Schoolyard Habitat Project Guide First Edition

Creating a School Habitat: A Planning Guide for Habitat Enhancement on School Grounds in Texas

Earth Partnership for Schools K-12 Curriculum Guide

Georgia Schoolyard Wildlife Habitat Planning Guide

**Design layout prepared by:** Pandion Systems, Inc. and J&S Design Studio

The guide can be downloaded from our website:
**http://www.fws.gov/cno/conservation/schoolyard.cfm**
The guide cannot be copied for resale. The guide can be copied for educational purposes. For more information, call 916/414-6464.


*Photos provided by the U.S. Fish & Wildlife Service (USFWS), Earth Partnership for Schools (EPS), Arlington Echo Outdoor School (AE), Lanthrop E. Smith Environmental Education Center (LSEEC) and Charles County Planning Division (CCPD).*

# Schoolyard Habitat Project Guide

## Table of Contents

## APPENDIX

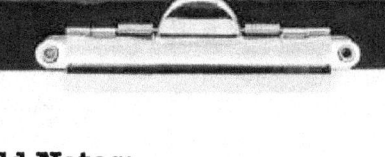

### Field Notes:

# About the Guide

## Welcome to your Schoolyard Habitat journey!

This is your guide book to transforming your school grounds into a place that engages the entire school community in habitat restoration. You are a part of a national movement dedicated to developing a citizenry that consciously values their environment. Once you move through this process, your school community will connect to the natural world, not by sitting inside and looking out, but instead by being outside and looking deeper.

This is a how-to guide. It will take you and your students through each step of the process: planning, installing and sustaining a project. This is not a book about why schoolyard projects are important; this is a guide about how to make the best one for your site.

There are important repeating images, themes and examples highlighted in this document:

### The Ripple Effect

A well designed Schoolyard Habitat project will have ripple effects on wildlife and people into the future, much like throwing a stone into a pond. To create your intended ripple effects, the initial stone thrown into your pond must be a well planned and ecologically sound project. The image of the stone thrown into the pond follows the three fundamental themes of a project to initiate, create and incorporate your project.

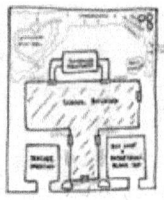

### Master Plan

A master plan is the vision of how your schoolyard could best be used by both wildlife and people. The plan can be formal or informal, but it is important to start with this step so you do not plant trees where future construction is planned. Once you have a master plan, you can easily break it down into phases, so each individual phase is part of a greater whole.

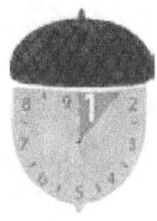

### The Steps

Schoolyard Habitat projects come in many different shapes and sizes and are very unique depending on the region and community in which they are created. However, there is a universal process that all projects go through. The sequential steps in this guide describe this process, ensuring you have all the tools necessary to complete a Schoolyard Habitat project. You will find many of the steps overlap, and you may need to consider the next step before finishing your current step. For that reason, we recommend you read through all of the steps before beginning.

### Projects

Throughout the guide, we talk about the ideal project pathway and then specific considerations for woodlands, meadows and wetlands. We realize that not all projects will fit into these classifications, and your region may use various terms to describe them. We use these terms to provide consistency throughout the guide, and as a way to help you make decisions; your project will ultimately be as unique as the wildlife and people that use it.

### Cityport Elementary School and Countryside High School

Stories and examples of these two schools are used throughout the guide. Cityport is an urban school with a small campus. Countryside High School is a suburban campus with open space and large sports fields. Both schools are based on real scenarios and are presented as models for you to create your own unique project.

### Field Notes

The Field Notes pages are designed to be removed and used in the field with students. We encourage you to incorporate these Field Notes into your existing school system curriculum to get your students outside as frequently as possible.

## A Few Notes About Your Journey

**You are not the first.**
This guide is a compilation of years of experience and thousands of projects from across the country and describes the fundamental elements of what makes great projects. Take comfort in this. Other people have successfully completed what you are starting; there are examples all over the nation.

**You are not alone.**
The U.S. Fish and Wildlife Service and many other agencies and organizations across the nation are dedicated to making projects like yours a reality. There is a common focus on developing programs to better connect our children, our communities and our natural world and on creating a new direction for our future.

**You have yet to realize where this will lead.**
Once you start this project, you will discover new things about yourself, your students, coworkers, community and environment. The world of Schoolyard Habitat projects is full of stories of awe, inspiration and motivation. You have yet to discover the people you will inspire to become leaders or the leader you will become. You are ready to begin!

## Keep the Focus on the Students

Students going outside frequently to learn, discover, create and celebrate is the ultimate goal of every Schoolyard Habitat. With that in mind, your students' involvement in and ownership of the Schoolyard Habitat site is the overarching element that must be present in all projects.

# U.S. Fish and Wildlife Service Schoolyard Habitat and Outdoor Classroom Program

The mission of the Schoolyard Habitat and Outdoor Classroom Program is to get students from across the country outside to experience nature. To accomplish this mission, the Program helps schools create natural spaces on school grounds where students will observe, draw, write, think and question.

A Schoolyard Habitat project restores native wildlife habitat, while an outdoor classroom area includes seating, tables and shade structures. Whether referred to as a Schoolyard Habitat or an outdoor classroom, all projects will benefit both wildlife and people and can range in size from a 1,000 square foot (sq ft) area to an acre or more. Regardless of the size and scope, all projects should be inspired and created by students and offer a place to learn outdoors.

In some schools and communities, developing a project on school grounds may not be possible. In these cases, you may be able to locate projects at nearby parks or other open areas; however, the process and concepts outlined in this guide should be applied to those locations as well.

A good Schoolyard Habitat project is ecologically sound, integrated into the curriculum and designed to encourage long-term stewardship. For a project to be sustainable, it must have active engagement from the larger school community, including parents, students, maintenance personnel and administrators.

Ecologically sound Schoolyard Habitat projects provide habitat for local and migratory wildlife, including songbirds, shorebirds, small mammals, reptiles, amphibians and insects. In many cases, these habitats also provide a vegetative buffer to nearby streams, reducing pollution reaching these waterways. To benefit the environment, the habitats must be significant enough in size and scope to have a lasting impact in the community.

Your Schoolyard Habitat project can offer teaching and learning opportunities across many academic disciplines. The process of planning, creating and using a habitat provides children with unique hands-on experiences. You do not have to limit the possibilities to just data collection for science. Remember that there are also opportunities to draw, write, research and much more.

During the formative years of life, students develop perceptions and values about their environment. If designed and managed properly, schoolyards can provide students with a powerful example of land conservation and stewardship. Experts know that young children are driven to explore, discover and play. A well designed schoolyard, including a diversity of natural areas, allows students to exercise these innate needs while nurturing their connection to nature.

USFWS

LSEEC

USFWS

*"The conservation of natural resources is the fundamental problem. Unless we solve that problem it will avail us little to solve all others."*

— *Theodore Roosevelt*

# INITIATE
## Steps 1 – 3

Perhaps you already have in mind what you want to do and how you want to do it. Or maybe you don't know exactly what you want; you simply know you want something different in your schoolyard. The first three steps create the foundation to ensure your project's success and sustainability. You and your students will be exploring and envisioning how wildlife and the school community will use the schoolyard into the future.

In these steps, you will create a team and a broad network of support. This team will define the size, scope and impact of the schoolyard project. The steps also outline the process to create a master plan and assess your project site. At the end of these three steps, you will have everything you need to create the best possible Schoolyard Habitat project.

The stone of your Schoolyard Habitat project will have lasting ripple effects—if you select the right stone, the right placement and the right people to throw it. Schoolyard Habitat projects have the ability to reconnect students and adults to the rhythms and patterns of our natural communities, while improving habitat for wildlife.

*"A true conservationist is a man who knows that the world is not given by his fathers, but borrowed from his children."*

— *John James Audubon*

## STEP ONE:
# Form a Team

Successful Schoolyard Habitat projects from across the country start with just one or two interested people at the school. A teacher, parent, community member or even a student can be the first person to get the ball rolling. But one person cannot complete a long-term successful project on his or her own.

The first step to creating a successful Schoolyard Habitat project is to organize a team that can provide support, resources and an overall stronger end product. Some teams are very formal with assigned duties and structure; others are casual with an informal approach to the project. All successful teams have a collaborative spirit and an agreed upon purpose.

The scope of the project and the professional climate of the school will influence the type of team needed to bring the project to successful completion.

**Accomplishments**

☑ Committed to Starting a Project

☑ Read Introduction

**Tasks**

☐ Establish Your Team

☐ Brainstorm Your Schoolyard Ideas

☐ Survey the School Community

☐ Brainstorm Potential Schoolyard Features

# Establish Your Team

Schoolyard Habitat teams are usually comprised of a core team that makes most of the decisions and a larger team of supportive helpers. The core team will motivate and push the direction of the project, while supportive helpers will take on individual tasks and assist in implementing the big events. Any of the following team members can be part of either team.

To generate interest and find members of your team, consider presenting at meetings, initiating casual conversations with other school community members or sending out a formal survey to your school community.

### Team members should include:

**Administrators:** Administrators can help ensure approval and garner school-wide support.

**Maintenance personnel:** The school maintenance supervisor and staff can provide insight into ideal site selection, (including the location of underground utilities), assistance with site prep and ongoing maintenance support.

**Students, teachers and parents:** The more people who take ownership of the project, the more successful it will be in the long term. Students, teachers and parents are all stakeholders with an interest in the appearance and use of the schoolyard.

**Community partners:** Community members, neighborhood associations and environmental organizations can offer technical expertise, assistance or donations for site prep, planting day supervision, ongoing maintenance and support for future projects.

**Natural resource professionals:** Contact your local county, state or federal natural resource office to find personnel who can help with the technical aspects of your project.

## Tips for Your Team

- Allow for varying levels of participation.

- Assign roles to help ensure that no one person is overburdened with all aspects of the project.

- Work within any existing formal committee structure of the school. Some very successful Schoolyard Habitat teams have been subcommittees of an overarching School Improvement Team or Parent Teacher Association.

- Identify achievable short-term goals. A simple, successful first project can create enthusiasm for future more complex projects.

- Have a flexible team roster so more people can join as they become interested.

- Designate a central location for your project files, so they can be located by current and future team members.

## Sample Schoolyard Habitat Team Roster

### CITYPORT ELEMENTARY SCHOOL

| Name | Role on Team | Role in School | Email & Phone | Description of Role |
|---|---|---|---|---|
| **Core Team – Processes information from student groups and administration into a cohesive plan.** | | | | |
| Asha Soni | Project Chairperson | Parent | | Organizes the project decision making, timeline and materials. |
| Tasha Hubbard | Communications Chairperson | 5th Grade Teacher | | Communicates the project steps. Involves all of her classes. |
| Ima Bank | Treasurer | 2nd Grade Teacher | | Creates and maintains the budget. Involves all of her classes. |
| **Supportive Team Members – Involved and consulted on all major decisions.** | | | | |
| Catherine Thompson | | Administrator | | Wants to be involved in all decision making. |
| Russell Sargent | Student Voice | Student | | Will write columns for the student newspaper and make posters. |
| M. Pat Moffett | Technical Assistance | Biologist | | Forester willing to assist with project design. |
| Logan Kelly | | 5th Grade Teacher | | Interested in helping, wants to know more. Used to work as a naturalist at a local park. |
| Ellen Brown | | Maintenance Person | | Has knowledge of the school's underground utilities. Coordinates the use of equipment. Wants to be involved in all decision making. |
| Margaret Silversmith | | Art Teacher | | Interested in helping, avid gardener and cross country coach. |
| Ron Fiorey | | Hardware Store Manager | | Graduated from the school. Interested in supporting the project. |

*As your project evolves and the tasks become more defined, each of the team members may take on different or additional roles.*

# Brainstorm Your Schoolyard Ideas

It is important to brainstorm why you want a Schoolyard Habitat before deciding what projects you want to create. Consider ways you will use your schoolyard in your curriculum. Refer to resources in the back of the guide for more ideas. For a project to be successful, you need to know how you want to use the project. Do not be concerned about limitations or barriers right now. The more students and adults you involve in this process, the richer the list of possibilities will be. You will refine these ideas to become the foundation of your school's master plan.

Have the team consider what they want to be able to do and see while outside. Then talk about other Schoolyard Habitat projects they have seen and what they liked about them. Consider the wildlife issues you want to address. It can be helpful to organize your thoughts into "Ideas for Wildlife" and "Ideas for People."

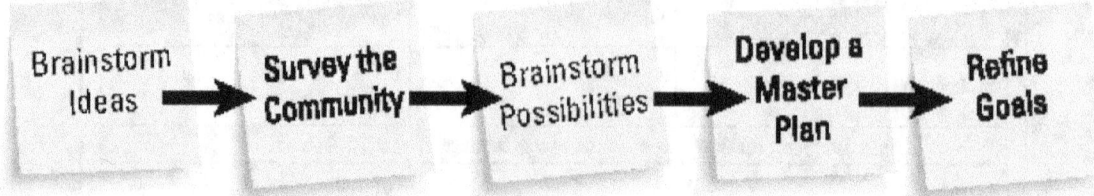

Brainstorm Ideas → Survey the Community → Brainstorm Possibilities → Develop a Master Plan → Refine Goals

**Sample of Brainstormed Schoolyard Habitat Ideas from Cityport Elementary School**

### Ideas for **Wildlife**

- Reduce storm-water runoff from rooftops.
- Create places for birds to nest.
- Enhance the grounds with trees and flowers.
- Support the entire life cycle of butterflies.

### Ideas for **People**

- Create a quiet space for students to read and do schoolwork outside.
- Provide opportunities for students to observe native birds and butterflies.
- Block some of the noise and sounds from the street.
- Develop shady areas near the playground.
- Create a trail to make younger students feel like they are exploring.

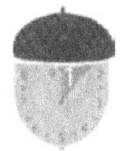

# Survey the School Community

The entire school community shares the same schoolyard, so it is important to understand the interests and concerns of the larger community. Find out what other members are thinking about; determine what others may or may not want changed. This is also a great way to bring more people and ideas into your plan so that the project will continue to be developed and used far into the future.

Here are a few ideas for surveying the school community:

- Post a schoolyard map with comment areas on a community bulletin board.
- Present and lead a faculty meeting discussion.
- Distribute an email or paper survey to staff, parents and students.
- Facilitate web-based discussions.
- Start and encourage informal office "water cooler" chats.
- Use school newsletters or message boards as a way to inform the school community.

---

**Sample Schoolyard Habitat Community Survey**

Good Morning Countryside High School!

The Schoolyard Habitat Team wants to improve the wildlife habitat value of our schoolyard. We are beginning our planning and would like to know your thoughts and ideas. Also, we are interested in knowing if you would like to join the team or have any skills that would be helpful. Please take a few moments to let us know the following:

How do you currently use the schoolyard? _____

How would you like to use your schoolyard differently than you do now? _____

What types of structures would be needed to help you use the schoolyard more often?_____

What types of wildlife would you like to see in the schoolyard? _____

What groups or individuals do you know of who use the schoolyard? _____

What parts of our schoolyard do you not want to see change? _____

What, if any, are your concerns about a Schoolyard Habitat project? _____

Are you interested in helping with our project? _____

Do you have any skills (such as carpentry, landscape design, gardening) that you would like to contribute to the project?_____
_____

Name: _____
Email: _____ Phone: _____

---

# Brainstorm Potential Schoolyard Possibilities

You have already begun to establish why you want a Schoolyard Habitat and who will be using it. Now is the time to start thinking about what features you want in your schoolyard. Web searches, fieldtrips to local habitat areas and discussions with other educators and natural resource professionals will provide many ideas. Networking with other teachers who have created a Schoolyard Habitat project is a great way to explore the possibilities for your own schoolyard.

Take the opportunity to immerse yourself and your team in examples of the habitat type you are attempting to restore on your school grounds. Bringing students on field trips to the natural settings is a powerful way to appreciate the significance of what you are trying to create on the school grounds. To find these examples and project support, contact U.S. Fish & Wildlife Service (USFWS) refuges and offices (**http://www.fws.gov/**) as well as other local environmental organizations.

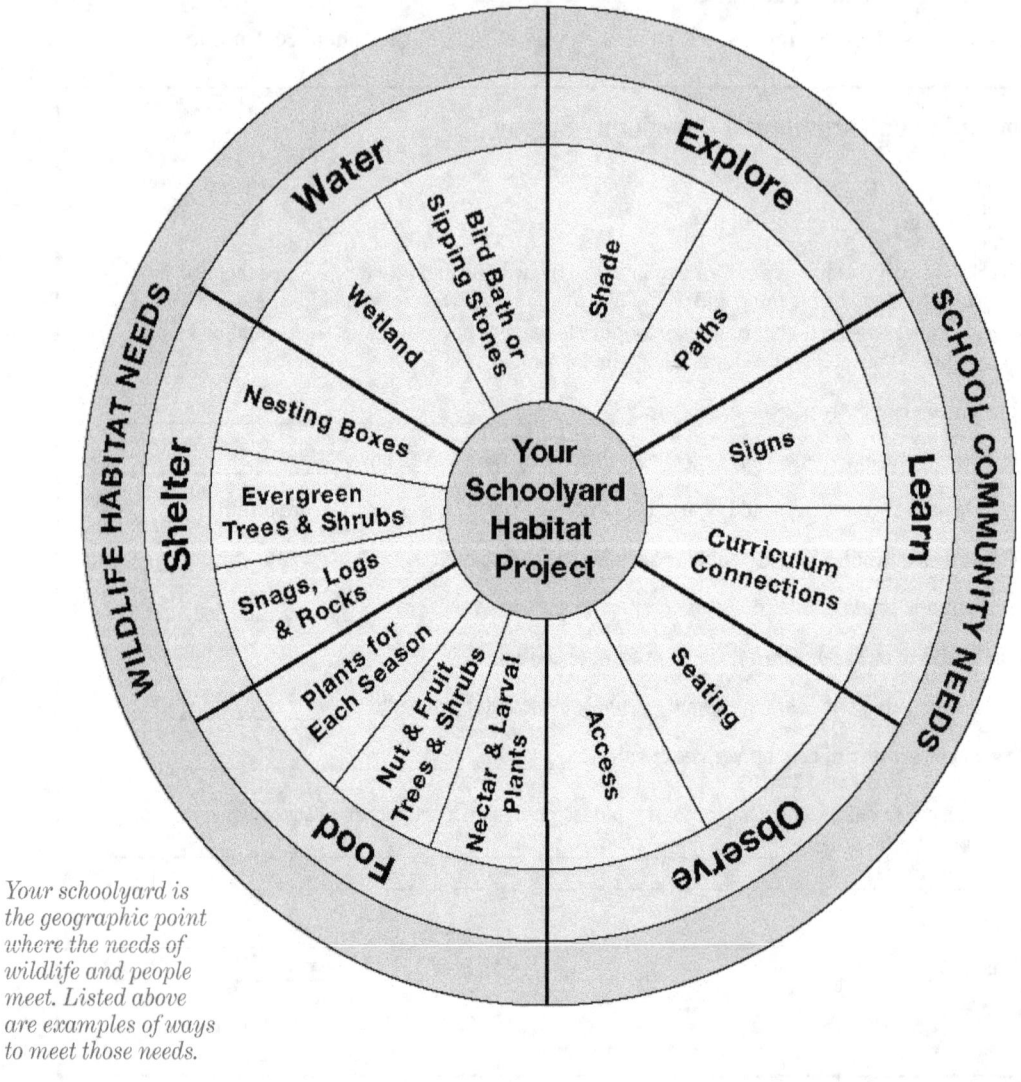

*Your schoolyard is the geographic point where the needs of wildlife and people meet. Listed above are examples of ways to meet those needs.*

Listed below are common types of Schoolyard Habitat projects and specific features. These ideas can be expanded upon or combined with others. Use these ideas and create your own list of what you would want in your schoolyard. There should be no limit to your team's imagination. With help and assistance, all projects are possible. To begin, brainstorm the types of habitat you would like to create, and then list the features you will incorporate. Large projects can be broken down into phases.

## Types of Habitat Projects

The most commonly replicated habitat types for your schoolyard are listed below. More details on each of these are found in the appendices.

### Woodland

Woodlands are areas dominated by large trees but also include many other plants, such as shrubs, small trees and herbaceous plants. Woodlands or forests have a canopy, midlayer, understory and floor. Each layer provides a wide range of food, shelter and space for many animals. A mature woodland floor is covered with decomposing leaves and trees. *Please refer to Appendix A for more information.*

### Meadow

Meadows are areas with tall grasses and wildflowers. In the central United States, meadows are referred to as prairies. In much of the rest of the United States meadows are transitional zones and if left alone would eventually evolve into a scrub-shrub habitat and then woodland. Meadows are known for their striking colors and textures. They provide dense cover for ground-nesting birds and burrowing animals and space for many insects including important pollinators. *Please refer to Appendix B for more information.*

### Wetland

All wetlands have three characteristics: water, saturated soil and plants adapted to wet conditions. Different types of wetlands are found in different regions of the United States including marshes, swamps, prairie potholes, and vernal pools. A marsh is the wettest type of wetland and is dominated by herbaceous plants such as cattails. A swamp is a wetland dominated by trees. Wetlands provide important habitat to many species as well as important water quality benefits. *Please refer to Appendix C for more information.*

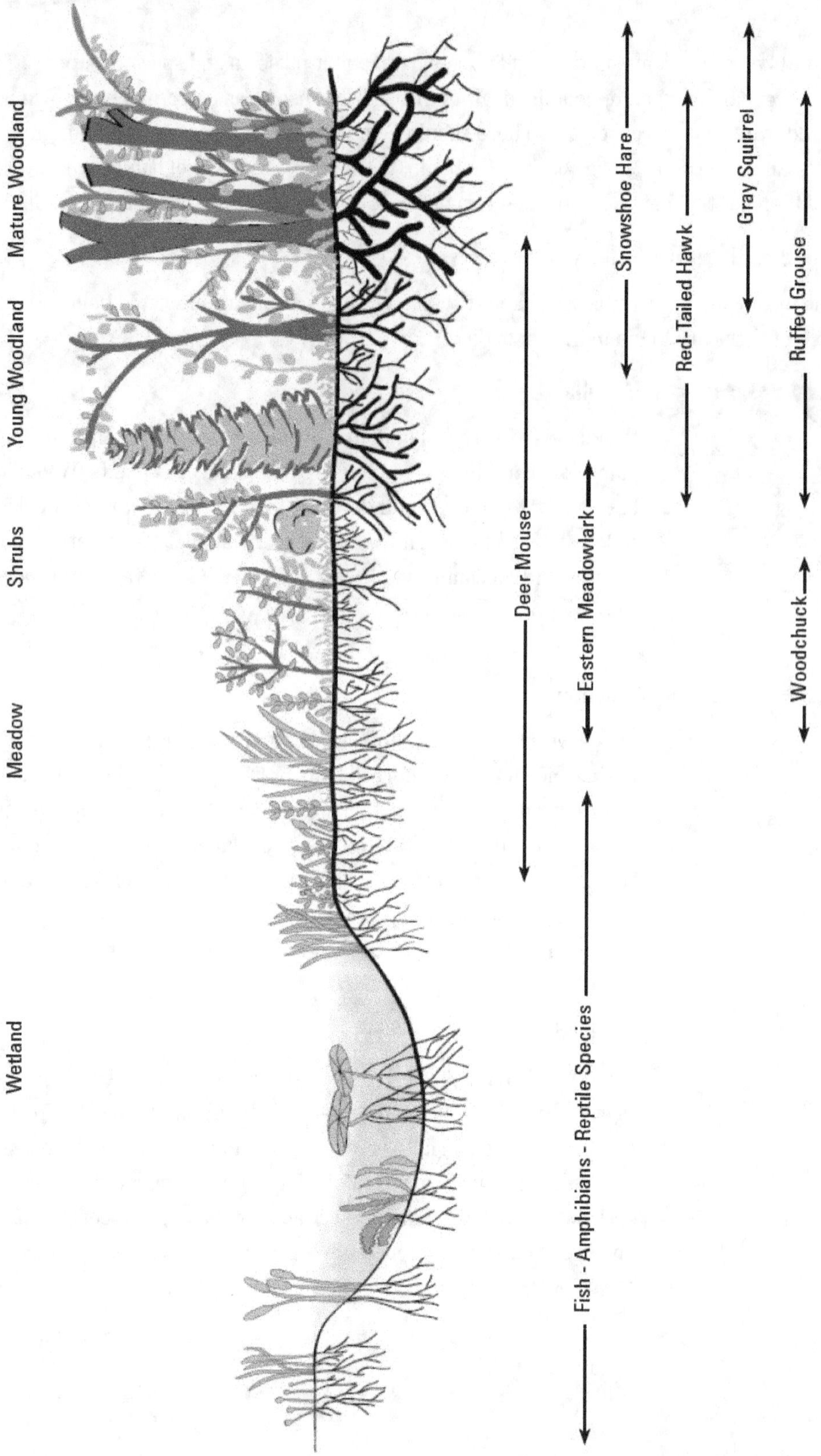

*Wildlife have naturally evolved to depend on certain habitats and the transition zones between them.*

Wetland    Meadow    Shrubs    Young Woodland    Mature Woodland

Snowshoe Hare

Red-Tailed Hawk

Gray Squirrel

Ruffed Grouse

Deer Mouse

Eastern Meadowlark

Woodchuck

Fish - Amphibians - Reptile Species

SCHOOLYARD HABITAT PROJECT GUIDE

## Additional Habitat Projects

Many land use innovations have incorporated native habitat restoration into creating gardens and water quality improvement projects. Depending on your region, you can also incorporate any of the following projects: raingardens, xeriscaping, bioswales, storm-water retention basins, hedgerows and windbreaks.

Gardens can be opportunities to explore specific curricular themes. Some of the many garden possibilities include berry patches, arboreta and gardens that focus on pollinators, hummingbirds or butterflies. Gardens can also have non-wildlife themes such as vegetable, storybook, sensory or herb gardens.

## Wildlife Features

**Logs:** Rotting logs provide habitat for many insects, amphibians and small mammals. Logs are good tools for learning the process of decay and the life associated with this process. Partially submerged logs in wetlands or ponds provide a place for turtles and frogs to bask.

**Snags:** Standing dead trees or snags provide nesting cavities for some birds like woodpeckers and chickadees, while insects living within the snags provide food for a variety of birds. Predatory birds, such as hawks, perch on snags for a better view of their prey.

**Brush Piles:** Brush piles in woodlands and along wooded edges provide excellent cover for rabbits, chipmunks, skunks, small birds and insects. Downed wood or discarded Christmas trees can be used to create brush piles.

**Nesting Boxes:** Nesting boxes for birds, bees, butterflies and bats are artificial structures that attract a greater variety of wildlife for students to observe.

## Accessibility

The structural integrity of any path, bridge or study area must be sound and in compliance with local codes and regulations, the Americans with Disabilities Act (ADA) and school district guidelines. Even when the parts and labor are donated, you are still creating infrastructure for the school, and it must be in compliance and inclusive of the entire community. Common materials for schoolyard nature trails are sod, decomposed granite or mulch and can easily meet the width, slope and firmness requirements for ADA. For more detailed information see **http://www.ada.gov/publicat.htm**.

USFWS

## School Community Features

These important elements invite people to use and interact with the natural world. *See Appendix D for sample designs of some of these features.*

**Trails:** Trails can be an excellent way for students to explore a habitat. They can be as simple as a mowed grass trail or more complex in design using decomposed granite or pavers.

**Seating and Study Platforms:** Create an outdoor work area for classes of students; it can be as simple as upside-down buckets, tree stumps or benches. A study platform or deck extending over a wetland edge will allow for student access, protect vegetation and limit wildlife disturbance.

*Having a formal entry way distinguishes your project as a place to go for inquiry and exploration.*

**Signs:** Signs encourage ownership, pride and understanding of the project. Signs can also help people understand the appearance of natural habitats.

**Fences:** Fences establish borders and are occasionally required by school systems depending on the project. If required to use a fence, use natural materials to improve its appearance.

**Shade Structure:** These features are great for providing a shady place to gather. Schools may have additional requirements if these structures are used for formal teaching.

**Wildlife Observation Blind:** A simple structure with a solid wooden wall with slats cut out at eye level will allow students to view wildlife on the other side. It should be placed in front of bird feeders, near wetlands or in meadows to observe secretive wildlife.

**Other Elements:** Wildlife tracking boxes, geology study areas, rain barrels, shade trees, natural playgrounds, weather stations, composting stations, greenhouses, sculptures, murals and other art projects are all worth considering.

# STEP TWO:
## Develop a Master Plan

In this step, you will walk the schoolyard and envision the placement of the projects and features that will transform your schoolyard. You will consider how water moves through the schoolyard, how wildlife and people use it and what parts of the schoolyard you have never considered before but hold great possibility. This will be your master plan. You will decide on a first project and establish an associated timeline.

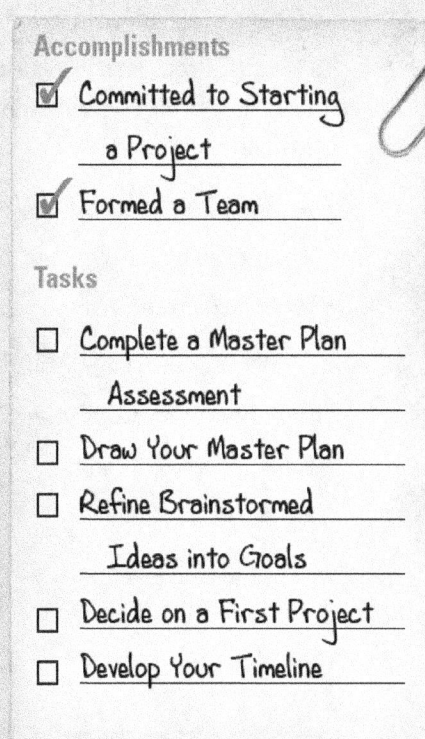

**Accomplishments**

- ☑ Committed to Starting a Project
- ☑ Formed a Team

**Tasks**

- ☐ Complete a Master Plan Assessment
- ☐ Draw Your Master Plan
- ☐ Refine Brainstormed Ideas into Goals
- ☐ Decide on a First Project
- ☐ Develop Your Timeline

# Complete a Master Plan Assessment

The master plan assessment is an important tool to help your team understand the entire schoolyard and its potential importance as both an education and wildlife resource.

To complete your master plan assessment, you and your students need to complete a schoolyard site survey as well as a schoolyard wildlife and habitat survey. A complete assessment includes looking at maps and walking the schoolyard a few times to form a broad perspective and collect details.

**The schoolyard site survey will identify the following:**

- Areas used by the students, both formally and informally
- Physical features that might influence the site of your project
- Areas that are off limits due to property lines or future expansions

**The schoolyard wildlife and habitat survey will identify the following:**

- Existing areas of habitat
- Evidence of wildlife use

## Wandering Water

Complete a schoolyard site survey after, or better yet, during a rain event. You will immediately see which way the water flows. Look for important details:

- Where has sediment collected?
- Where is water standing?

You can use this natural flow of water in your Schoolyard Habitat project.

USFWS

*These master plan assessments form the basis for the master plans and help identify initial schoolyard projects.*

## Example of a Master Plan Assessment: Cityport Elementary School

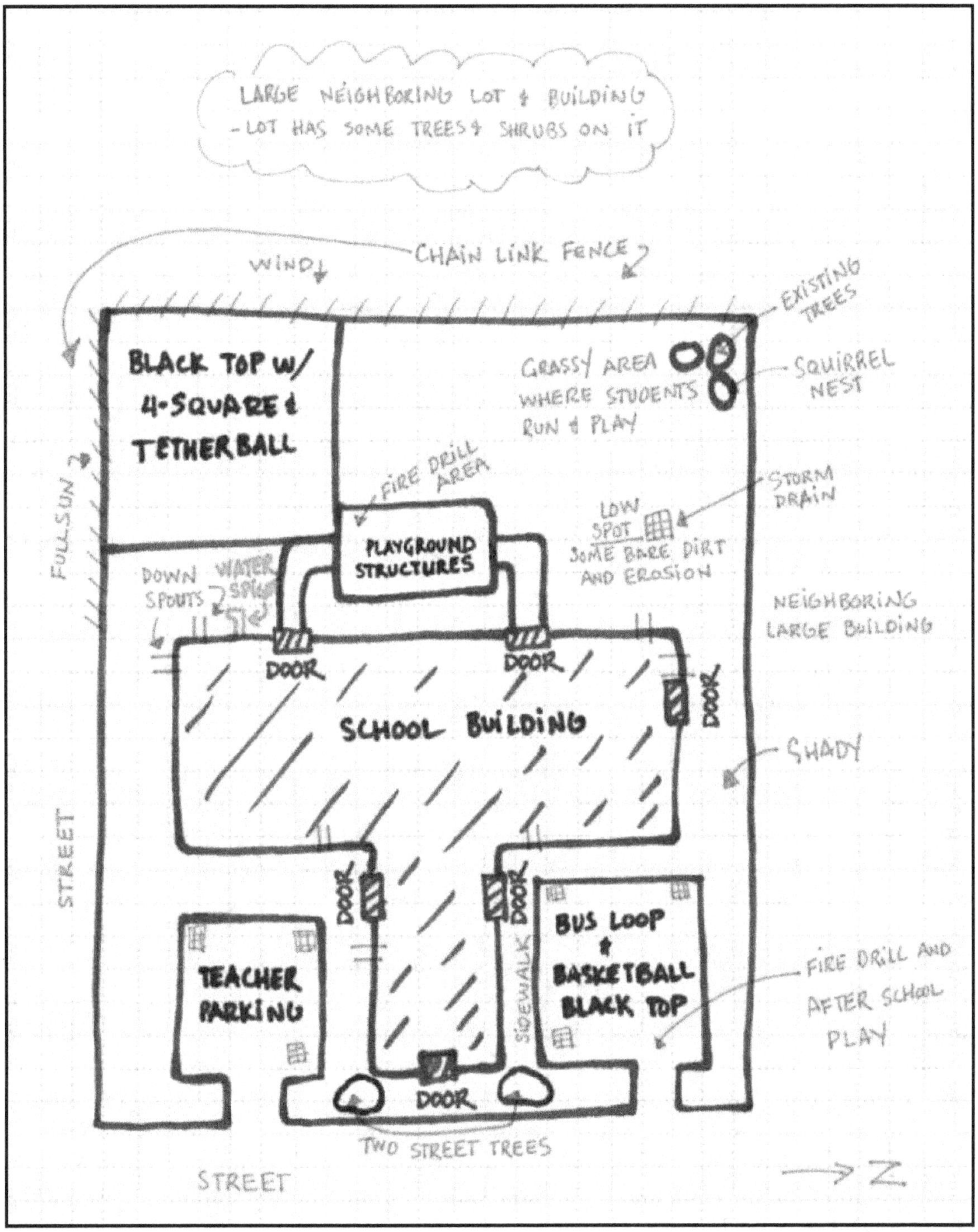

LARGE NEIGHBORING LOT & BUILDING - LOT HAS SOME TREES & SHRUBS ON IT

CHAIN LINK FENCE

WINDS

EXISTING TREES

BLACK TOP W/ 4-SQUARE & TETHERBALL

GRASSY AREA WHERE STUDENTS RUN & PLAY

SQUIRREL NEST

FULL SUN

FIRE DRILL AREA

STORM DRAIN

LOW SPOT SOME BARE DIRT AND EROSION

PLAYGROUND STRUCTURES

DOWN SPOUTS

WATER SPIG

NEIGHBORING LARGE BUILDING

DOOR

DOOR

DOOR

SCHOOL BUILDING

SHADY

STREET

DOOR

SIDEWALK DOOR

BUS LOOP & BASKETBALL BLACK TOP

FIRE DRILL AND AFTER SCHOOL PLAY

TEACHER PARKING

DOOR

TWO STREET TREES

STREET

→ Z

## Example of a Master Plan Assessment: Countryside High School

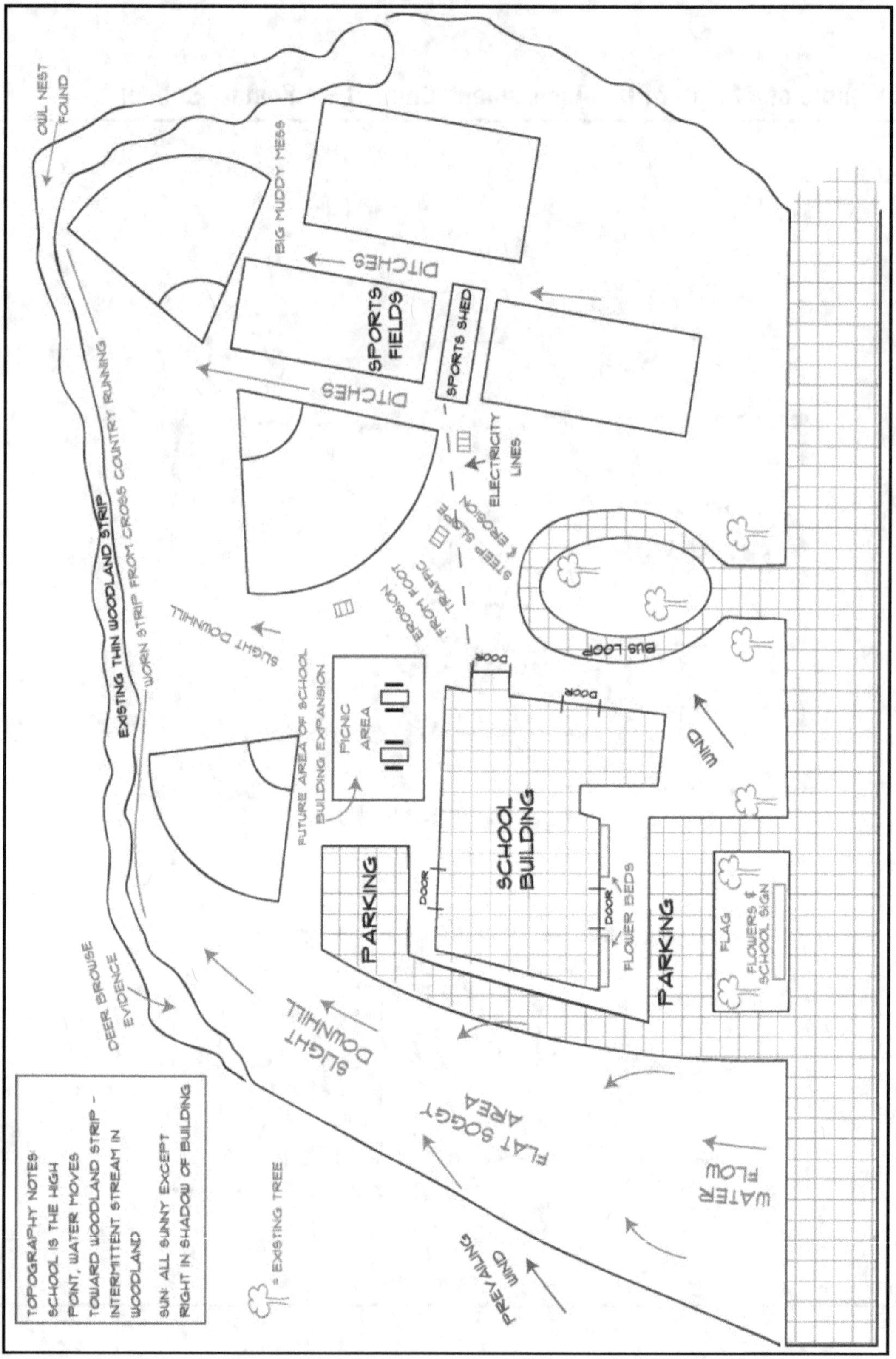

TOPOGRAPHY NOTES:
SCHOOL IS THE HIGH POINT, WATER MOVES TOWARD WOODLAND STRIP - INTERMITTENT STREAM IN WOODLAND

SUN: ALL SUNNY EXCEPT RIGHT IN SHADOW OF BUILDING

= EXISTING TREE

OWL NEST FOUND

BIG MUDDY MESS

DITCHES

SPORTS FIELDS

SPORTS SHED

DITCHES

ELECTRICITY LINES

EROSION

STEEP SLOPE

EROSION FROM FOOT TRAFFIC

BUS LOOP

DOOR

SLIGHT DOWNHILL

EXISTING THIN WOODLAND STRIP

WORN STRIP FROM CROSS COUNTRY RUNNING

DEER BROWSE EVIDENCE

FUTURE AREA OF SCHOOL BUILDING EXPANSION

PICNIC AREA

WIND

SCHOOL BUILDING

DOOR

PARKING

DOOR

FLOWER BEDS

DOOR

PARKING

FLAG FLOWERS & SCHOOL SIGN

SLIGHT DOWNHILL

FLAT SOGGY AREA

WATER FLOW

PREVAILING WIND

## Schoolyard Site Survey

**Tools for Schoolyard Site Survey:**

- Copies of Field Notes for Completing a Schoolyard Site Survey

- All available maps and images of the school

- Your team, including your maintenance and natural resource professionals

- Camera, measuring tape, field guide and binoculars

**Types of Maps and Images:**

- An aerial photo will help identify important features such as existing wildlife corridors and nearby rivers and streams.

- Soil surveys indicate the types of soil found on a site and will help you identify which plant species and habitat projects would be appropriate on the school grounds.

- Topographical maps identify the steep slopes and flat areas on your campus which will help in the placement of projects.

- Building plans indicate important information such as property lines, plans for future expansion and school maintained utilities.

## Where to Find Maps

Many of these maps and images can be found using online search engines or by visiting school district and county planning offices.
The U.S. Department of Agriculture Farm Service Agency **http://www.fsa.usda.gov** and the Natural Resources Conservation Service **http://www.nrcs.usda.gov/** may be able to supply additional information.

Cindy Landers

## Schoolyard Wildlife and Habitat Survey

A schoolyard wildlife and habitat survey is an evaluation of what wildlife uses your schoolyard. This survey will establish the baseline data for your team to track changes over time.

Repeat this same data collection method over the course of several years as the project is planned, installed and maintained. Consider where and how the information will be stored and preserved, as well as ways to share the data online or in another public forum. Be aware that collecting data at varying times of the year can result in different data.

Your wildlife and habitat survey data will influence the selection and placement of a project. For example, at Cityport Elementary School, their team was considering creating a native plant garden at the front of the school. After completing their habitat survey, they discovered that no birds or butterflies seemed to visit the front of the school. However, they did observe three different species of butterflies and moths in the back of the school. They decided to help support these visitors by making sure their first project included additional native nectar plants for pollinators as well as a woodland to attract birds.

## Methods for Data Collection

### Photo points

Establish a photo point by hammering a wooden post into the corner of a plot on your site. Mark each site with an identifying name to help catalogue photos. Make notes and keep them with the photos. Consider recording an audio clip to attach to the photo.

### Single spot observations

Similar to a photo point, students identify and return regularly to their own individual spots on the schoolyard to record their observations. Student "single-spots" should be at least 10 feet apart from each other. The more often they do this exercise the richer their observations become.

### Transects

Use hula-hoops or other fixed shapes as a technique to survey and record plant and insect data across the project site.

### Discovering Diversity

Noticing the diversity of insects, birds and plants is more important than knowing the names of each one. Do not be intimidated by any lack of experience or knowledge. Learning and discovering alongside your students is very powerful for both you and your students.

Frank Marsden

# Field Notes for Completing a Schoolyard Site Survey

## Procedure:

1. Draw an outline of the school property, school buildings and parking lots. This is your base map.
2. Break into groups and walk the entire schoolyard.
3. Sketch on your base map all of the important physical, human-related and biological characteristics listed below. Create a legend and designate symbols to mark important characteristics.
4. Share your observations as a class.
5. Create a collective schoolyard site survey.

### Physical Characteristics

**Topography:**

- Identify high and low spots.
- Locate steep slopes.

**Prevailing wind:**

- Indicate prevailing wind direction.

**Sunny and shady areas:**

- Distinguish between areas that receive full sun, partial shade and full shade.

**Water:**

- Designate any areas that are obvious drainage or waterways.
- Indicate direction of water runoff.
- Locate any areas where erosion is occurring.
- Locate spots that seem especially wet or dry.

### Human-Related Characteristics

**Structures:**

- Identify structures where students play or gather such as playground equipment, bike racks, signs, benches, picnic tables and fences.

**Fields:**

- Identify the athletic fields and areas that are used for informal play either by the school or other members of the community.
- Identify where students gather for fire drills.

**Accessibility:**

- Identify areas that are accessible during a class period.
- Indicate formal and informal pathways.
- Identify spaces used by the public.

**Utility features:**

- Locate obvious utility lines above or below ground.
- Locate existing water or irrigation lines and accessible spigots.

### Biological Characteristics

**Plants:**

- Locate and identify trees, shrubs and plants that provide food and cover for wildlife, both on and adjacent to the school grounds.

**Wildlife:**

- Locate and identify signs of wildlife on the school grounds.

**Groundcover:**

- Indicate different groundcovers such as turf grass, bare spots, pavement, woodland groundcovers, native plantings or garden areas.

*"There is a way that nature speaks, that land speaks. Most of the time we are simply not patient enough, quiet enough, to pay attention to the story."*

— *Linda Hogan*

# Field Notes for Completing a Schoolyard Wildlife and Habitat Survey

**Procedure:**

1. Record the date and time.
2. Sit at least a full arms length away from anyone else.
3. Silently observe for 10 minutes.
4. Record observation on the wildlife survey.
5. Share observations.
6. Complete habitat survey with your class.

## Wildlife Survey

- Listen and look for signs of wildlife.
- Identify and describe an animal you see or one of its signs.
- Draw a picture of it.
- Describe how it changes throughout the day.

## Habitat Survey

- List wildlife food you find.
- List water sources for wildlife you see.
- List the hiding places for insects, birds and mammals you find.
- List other evidence of wildlife you discover such as tracks, feathers, nests or droppings.

When searching for schoolyard wildlife,

be quiet and respectful and you will find even more!

*"Nature will bear the closest inspection. She invites us to lay our eye level with her smallest leaf, and take an insect view of its plain."*

— *Henry David Thoreau*

# Draw Your Master Plan

Your drawing can be very informal and should be done with your students. A master plan can continue to evolve and change as the projects are implemented. It allows for large projects to be broken down into phases, and each phase can be celebrated as a success story. This phased approach can allow for future students to be involved with project site assessment, design and creation.

## Method for Drawing a Master Plan

- Consider all the brainstormed schoolyard features and ideas for use from Step 1.
- Review your master plan assessment and indicate the best possible location for features.
- Review the drawing and consider the location of your projects and their accessibility to student use and watering.
- Use a collaborative process to create your master plan, incorporating the ideas of both team members and students.

*Below are two master plans based on their schoolyard site surveys. Countryside's master plan was created by their landscape architect class, while Cityport's master plan was drawn by the lead teachers.*

## Example of a Master Plan: Cityport Elementary School

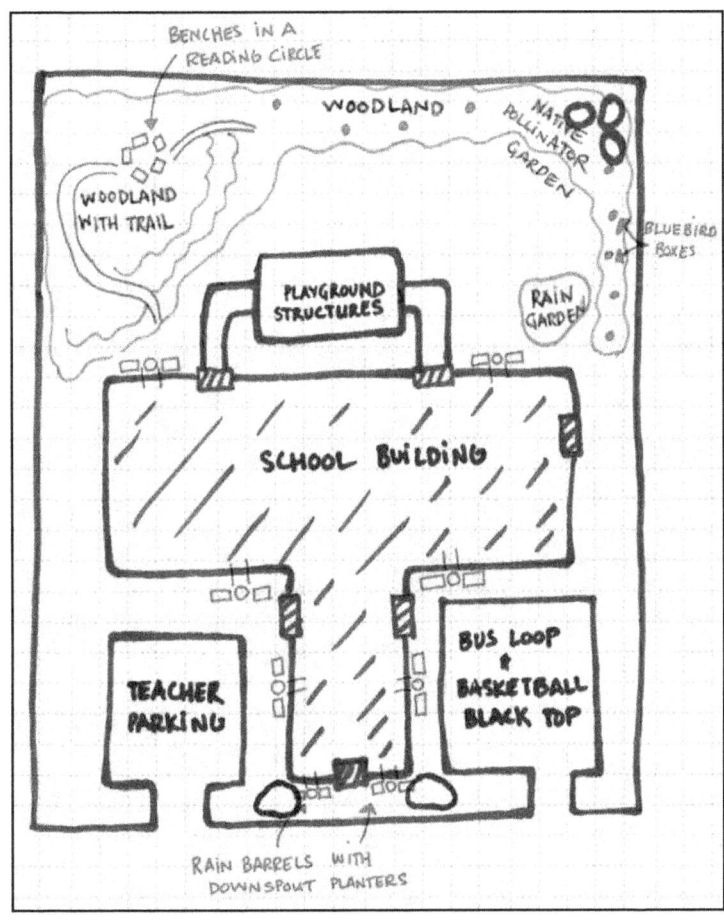

## Example of a Master Plan: Countryside High School

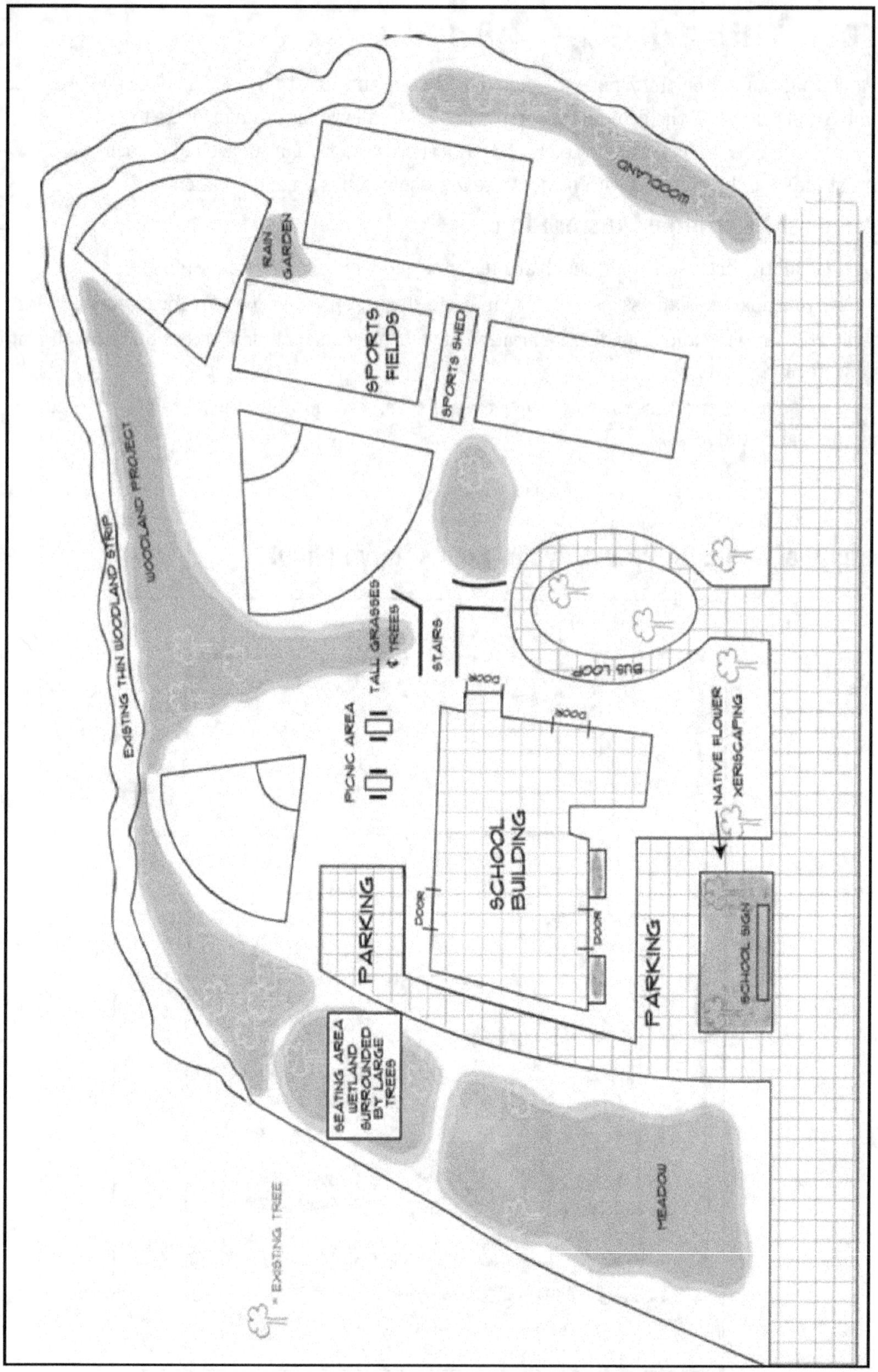

WOODLAND

RAIN GARDEN

SPORTS FIELDS

SPORTS SHED

EXISTING THIN WOODLAND STRIP

WOODLAND PROJECT

TALL GRASSES & TREES

STAIRS

PICNIC AREA

DOOR

DOOR

BUS LOOP

SCHOOL BUILDING

DOOR

DOOR

DOOR

PARKING

NATIVE FLOWER XERISCAPING

PARKING

SCHOOL SIGN

SEATING AREA WETLAND SURROUNDED BY LARGE TREES

= EXISTING TREE

MEADOW

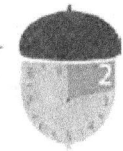

# Refine Brainstormed Ideas into Goals

The goals should be clearly written so that future team members will understand the purpose of the master plan. Well defined goals help keep the project focused and decision making easier throughout the design, implementation and use.

*The process of refining ideas into goals for Cityport Elementary School.*

**Brainstormed Ideas for Wildlife**

- Reduce storm-water runoff from the rooftops.
- Create places for birds to nest.
- Enhance the grounds with trees and flowers.
- Support the entire life cycle of butterflies.

**Refined Goals for Wildlife**

- Establish a schoolyard woodland by planting 5,000 sq ft of locally native trees over the course of two years.
- Create a native plant pollinator garden, that will double the observed species of pollinators within two years.
- Establish and maintain a bluebird box trail.
- Reduce the volume of storm-water runoff from rooftops by 20%.

**Brainstormed Ideas for People**

- Create a quiet space for students to read and do schoolwork outside.
- Provide opportunity for students to observe native birds and butterflies.
- Block some of the noise and sounds from the street.
- Develop shady areas near the playground.
- Create a trail to make younger students feel like they are exploring.

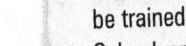

**Refined Goals for People**

- All grade level teachers will be trained in the uses of the Schoolyard Habitat.
- Compile student observations into an annual schoolyard species count of bird and insect populations.
- Provide a private oasis in our schoolyard for students to read, write and reflect.

# Decide on a First Project

Look at your entire master plan and list of goals. Decide what you want to do first. Break down your goals and projects into phases. By the time you complete the phases of your master plan, all of your goals should be accomplished. Be sure that all of your team members agree, especially the administration and maintenance personnel. This will help ensure project success.

*Cityport Elementary School's project master plan broken down into phases.*

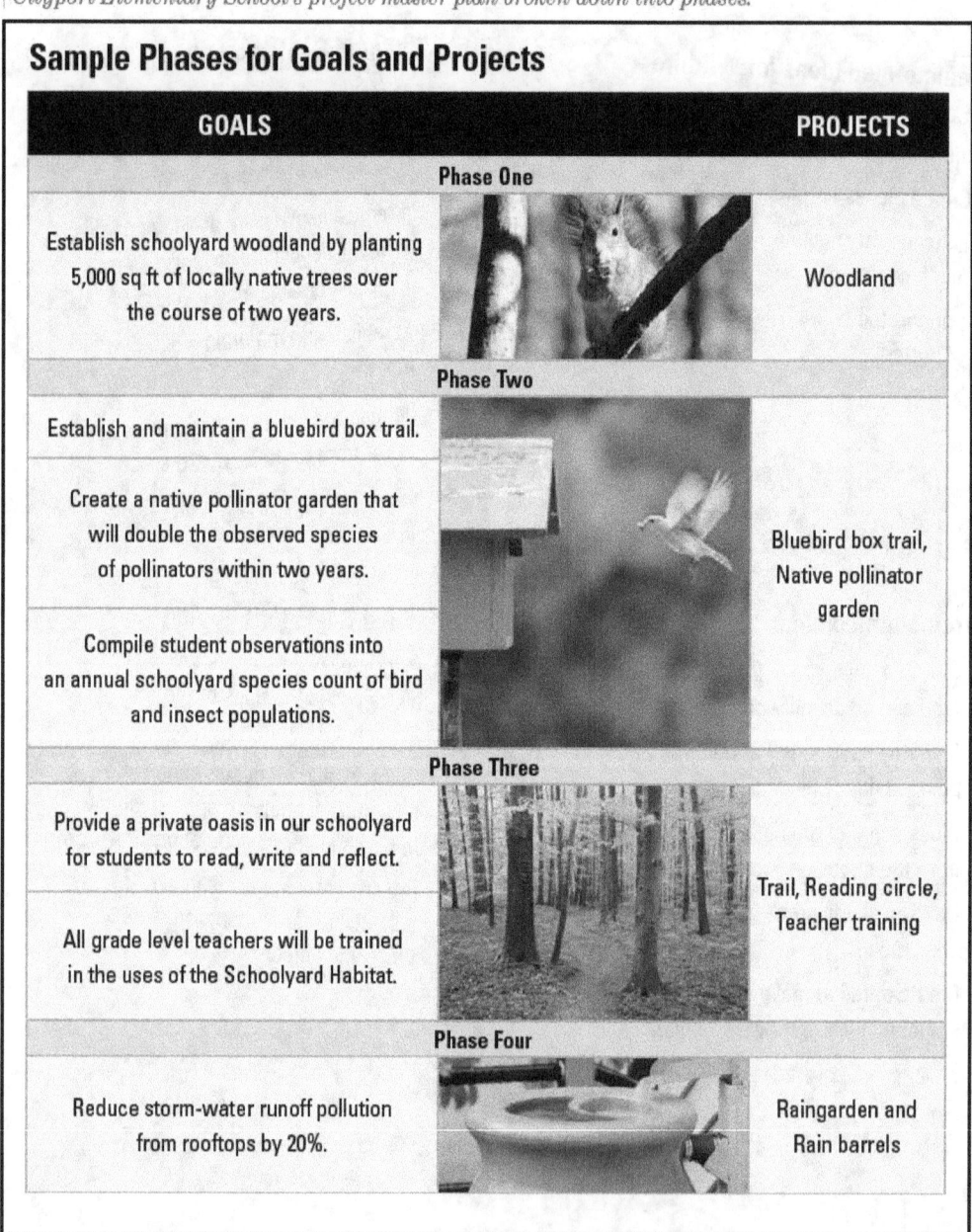

**Sample Phases for Goals and Projects**

| GOALS | PROJECTS |
|---|---|
| **Phase One** | |
| Establish schoolyard woodland by planting 5,000 sq ft of locally native trees over the course of two years. | Woodland |
| **Phase Two** | |
| Establish and maintain a bluebird box trail. | |
| Create a native pollinator garden that will double the observed species of pollinators within two years. | Bluebird box trail, Native pollinator garden |
| Compile student observations into an annual schoolyard species count of bird and insect populations. | |
| **Phase Three** | |
| Provide a private oasis in our schoolyard for students to read, write and reflect. | |
| All grade level teachers will be trained in the uses of the Schoolyard Habitat. | Trail, Reading circle, Teacher training |
| **Phase Four** | |
| Reduce storm-water runoff pollution from rooftops by 20%. | Raingarden and Rain barrels |

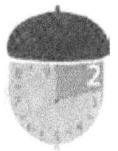

# Develop Your Timeline

Now that you know what project you will be working on, you need to develop a timeline. This will help organize the many tasks associated with your project. It will also help you communicate to others what needs to be accomplished and when. Your timeline should include all the steps in this guide. These steps will overlap. For example, you might be working on assessing your project site (Step 3) while still recruiting new team members (Step 1).

*Most projects take 18 months to progress from the first idea to planting day. Begin by choosing a proposed planting date that falls immediately before or during seasonal rains.*

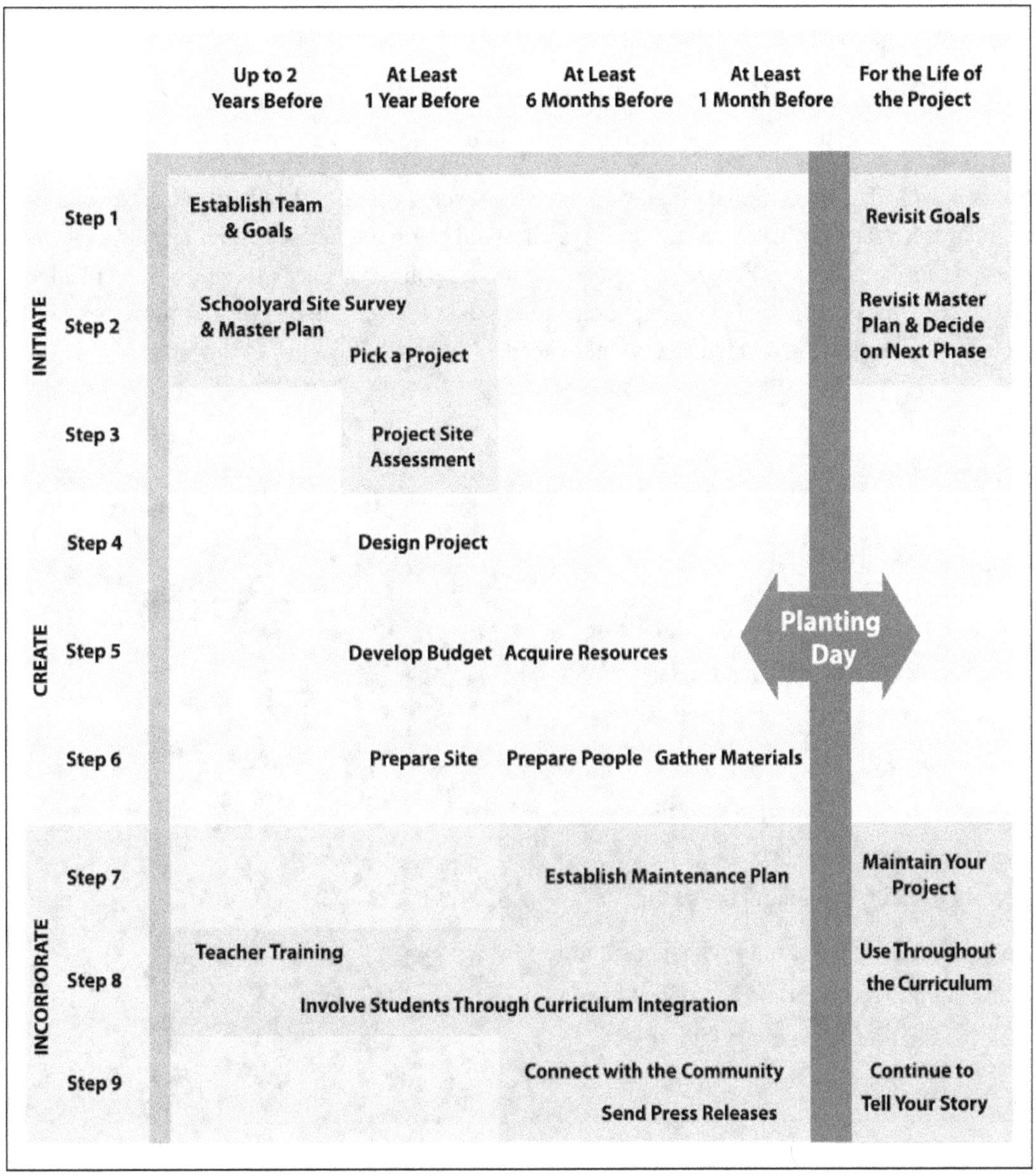

| | | Up to 2 Years Before | At Least 1 Year Before | At Least 6 Months Before | At Least 1 Month Before | For the Life of the Project |
|---|---|---|---|---|---|---|
| **INITIATE** | Step 1 | Establish Team & Goals | | | | Revisit Goals |
| | Step 2 | Schoolyard Site Survey & Master Plan | Pick a Project | | | Revisit Master Plan & Decide on Next Phase |
| | Step 3 | | Project Site Assessment | | | |
| **CREATE** | Step 4 | | Design Project | | | |
| | Step 5 | | Develop Budget | Acquire Resources | | |
| | Step 6 | | Prepare Site | Prepare People | Gather Materials | |
| **INCORPORATE** | Step 7 | | | Establish Maintenance Plan | | Maintain Your Project |
| | Step 8 | Teacher Training | Involve Students Through Curriculum Integration | | | Use Throughout the Curriculum |
| | Step 9 | | | Connect with the Community | Send Press Releases | Continue to Tell Your Story |

**Planting Day**

## Revise Your Timeline

Your planting day should be non-intrusive to the school schedule, so the majority of students can be involved. Have a few possible planting dates to allow for inclement weather or unexpected school events. As you move through the project site assessment and design, you may need to revisit and revise your timeline. Consider how Cityport Elementary School created and revised their timeline.

**Make timeline:** Cityport Elementary School's habitat team decided they wanted to create a woodland for Arbor Day this year. They identified Arbor Day as a good time to plant trees and could involve the whole student community. The team worked backward from this day to determine when they needed to talk with a forester and gather supplies. They also worked forward from this day to establish how they would use and maintain the site.

**Move forward:** The team discovered after working with a forester that their woodland was a great project for the school site; however, it would take an additional year to do proper ground preparation.

**Revise the plan:** The team decided that some members would continue working on the woodland to be the following year's project. The rest of the team would begin the native pollinator garden from their project master plan for this year's project. The native pollinator garden would still be planted on Arbor Day. Having a project master plan, team and timeline allowed the projects to move forward and the team to stay focused, motivated and accomplished.

## Tips for Your Timeline

- Allow adequate time to achieve each step, particularly time for unexpected delays in the project approval or implementation.

- Schoolyard Habitat teams naturally lag during summer months and around the holidays. Keep your timeline realistic and adjust for your availability throughout the year.

- Be flexible. Sometimes entire timelines and plans need to be reworked and revised as your team learns more about the project.

# STEP THREE:
## Assess Project Site

The information you gather here is for your first project site and will provide the information you need to complete a successful project design. This is another great opportunity to get your students outside. The two main parts of the project site assessment is measuring the project area and assessing growing conditions.

**Accomplishments**

- ☑ Committed to Starting a Project
- ☑ Formed a Team
- ☑ Developed a Master Plan

**Tasks**

- ☐ Measure Project Area
- ☐ Assess Growing Conditions

3

*"No shade tree?  Blame not the sun but yourself."*

— *Chinese Proverb*

# Measure Project Area

To determine the amount of materials you need for your project site, you will first determine the size of the project area in square feet. Although your project is probably not rectangular or square in shape you can still use the following calculation to get an estimate, or have the students take a more accurate measurement as a math activity. To do this, place stakes or pin flags around the perimeter of the project area; then have students estimate and measure the area. You will be using this number throughout the rest of the project design and installation.

$$\text{Area in ft}^2 \text{ (A)} = \text{Length in ft x Width in ft}$$

# Assess Growing Conditions

There are four essential elements to your project site's growing conditions: sunlight, existing vegetation, water and soil. Observing your site at different times of the day and year allows you to collect data that will support a stronger project design.

## Sunlight

The duration of sunlight throughout the day determines the species of plants that can thrive on the site. The length and intensity of sunlight will allow you to decide whether a shade structure or tall trees are needed.

## Existing Vegetation

Assess what is currently growing on and adjacent to your project site. This will impact the type of ground preparation and maintenance required. For example, if the area adjacent to your site is dominated by an invasive non-native vine, then you will need to develop a plan to manage that vine as part of your project.

## Water

Average annual rainwater and storm-water flow on your site will determine the plants that will thrive there as well as any watering needs.

## Soil

Soil texture and infiltration will help you determine what type of soil occurs at your site. Texture and infiltration indicate the type of plants that would naturally grow there as well as if soil amendments are needed to support your project. For example, if your site is dominated by clay soils and you are planning a wetland, you may not have to add soil amendments.

## Soil Infiltration

Infiltration will indicate how hard your soil is. Soil can be quite hard due to compaction or heavy clay content. If so, you may want to use an auger or other machinery to help get the holes started before planting day.

EPS

*Below are the student generated project site assessments for Cityport Elementary School and Countryside High School.*

## Example of a Project Site Assessment: Cityport Elementary School

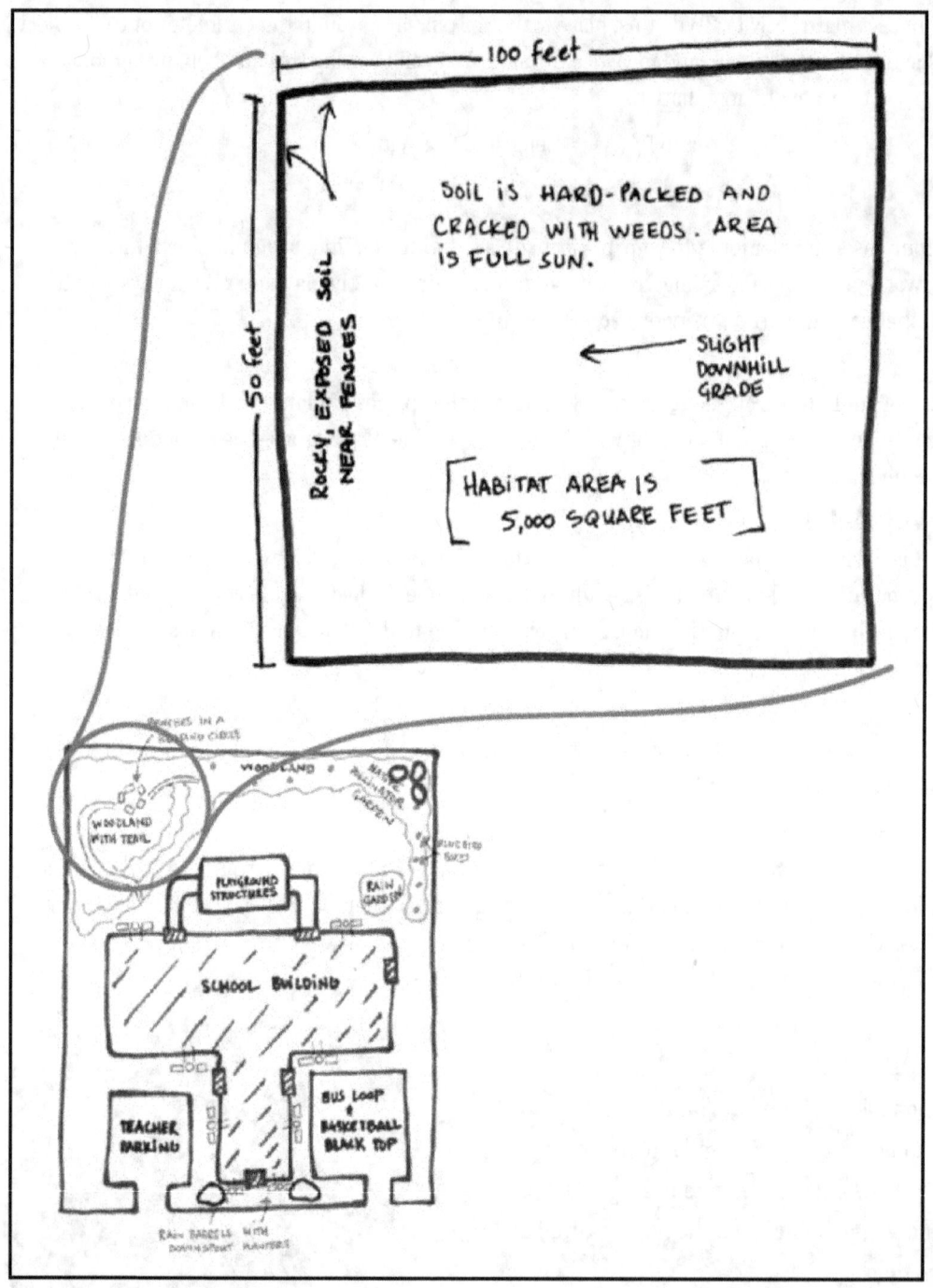

## Example of a Project Site Assessment: Countryside High School

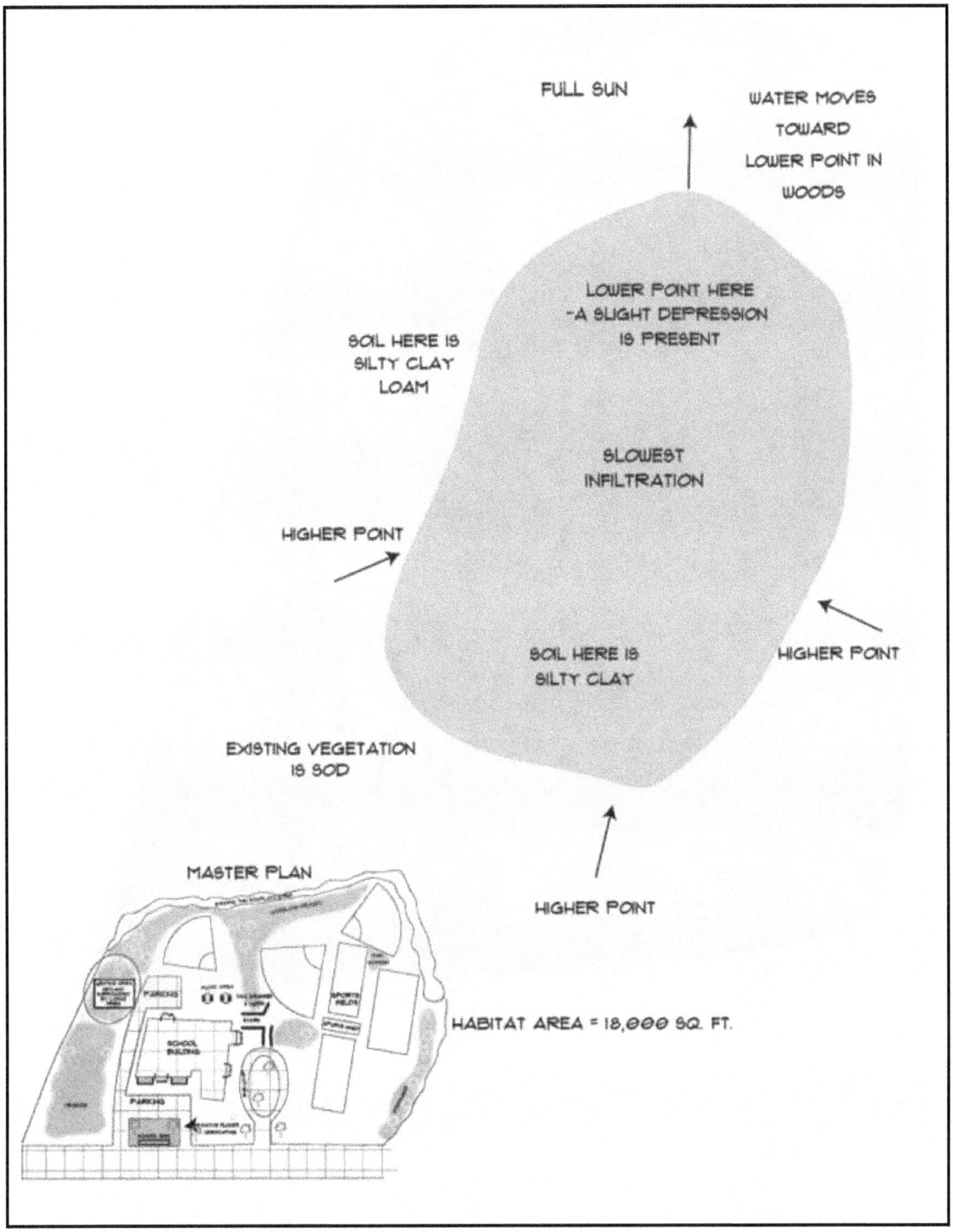

FULL SUN

WATER MOVES
TOWARD
LOWER POINT IN
WOODS

LOWER POINT HERE
-A SLIGHT DEPRESSION
IS PRESENT

SOIL HERE IS
SILTY CLAY
LOAM

SLOWEST
INFILTRATION

HIGHER POINT

SOIL HERE IS
SILTY CLAY

HIGHER POINT

EXISTING VEGETATION
IS SOD

MASTER PLAN

HIGHER POINT

PARKING

SCHOOL
BUILDING

PARKING

HABITAT AREA = 18,000 SQ. FT.

*"I believe a leaf of grass is no less than the journey-work of the stars."*

— *Walt Whitman*

# Field Notes for Soil Assessment

## Soil Texture Procedure:

1. Gather materials: soil auger, small cup of water.

2. Use a soil auger to access soil at least 12 inches below the surface.

3. Follow the directions on the chart below to determine soil texture.

4. Repeat at several locations within your project site and record any differences observed.

## Soil Infiltration Procedure:

1. Gather materials: shovel, cups of water, stop watch, clipboard, paper, pencil.

2. Dig a hole 6 inches deep.

3. Pour one cup of water into the hole.

4. Record how long it takes for the water to infiltrate.

5. Repeat at several locations within your project site and record any differences observed.

# Soil Texture Chart

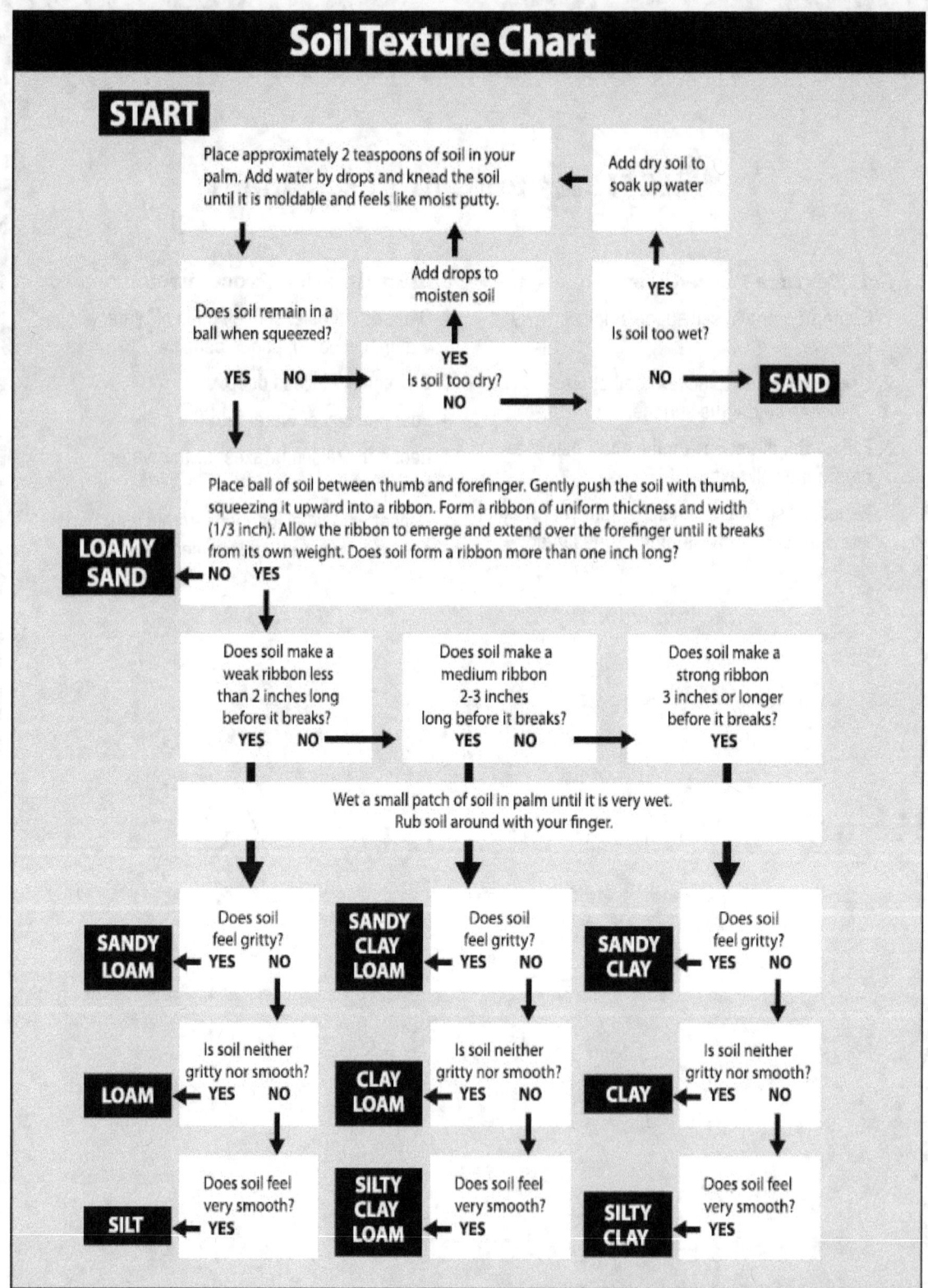

**START**

Place approximately 2 teaspoons of soil in your palm. Add water by drops and knead the soil until it is moldable and feels like moist putty.

Add dry soil to soak up water

Does soil remain in a ball when squeezed?

Add drops to moisten soil

**YES** Is soil too wet?

**YES** **NO** ➔

**YES** Is soil too dry?

**NO** ➔

**NO** ➔ **SAND**

Place ball of soil between thumb and forefinger. Gently push the soil with thumb, squeezing it upward into a ribbon. Form a ribbon of uniform thickness and width (1/3 inch). Allow the ribbon to emerge and extend over the forefinger until it breaks from its own weight. Does soil form a ribbon more than one inch long?

**LOAMY SAND** ⬅ **NO** **YES**

Does soil make a weak ribbon less than 2 inches long before it breaks?
**YES** **NO** ➔

Does soil make a medium ribbon 2-3 inches long before it breaks?
**YES** **NO** ➔

Does soil make a strong ribbon 3 inches or longer before it breaks?
**YES**

Wet a small patch of soil in palm until it is very wet. Rub soil around with your finger.

Does soil feel gritty?
**SANDY LOAM** ⬅ **YES** **NO**

Does soil feel gritty?
**SANDY CLAY LOAM** ⬅ **YES** **NO**

Does soil feel gritty?
**SANDY CLAY** ⬅ **YES** **NO**

Is soil neither gritty nor smooth?
**LOAM** ⬅ **YES** **NO**

Is soil neither gritty nor smooth?
**CLAY LOAM** ⬅ **YES** **NO**

Is soil neither gritty nor smooth?
**CLAY** ⬅ **YES** **NO**

Does soil feel very smooth?
**SILT** ⬅ **YES**

Does soil feel very smooth?
**SILTY CLAY LOAM** ⬅ **YES**

Does soil feel very smooth?
**SILTY CLAY** ⬅ **YES**

*Adapted with permission from Environmental Concern, Inc.*

# CREATE
## Steps 4 – 6

You are now about to transform the appearance of your school grounds. The following steps are the heart of your Schoolyard Habitat project. This is where hands get dirty and the land is transformed. You will be considering all the practical aspects which include the design, cost and tools for the project.

This is the most technically complex section and therefore the longest part of the guide. It may take longer than one academic year to complete all three steps. This is also the part where student involvement can sometimes become overshadowed by the enthusiasm of the adults involved. It is important to keep the students engaged on every level as you move through these steps. Stay focused on why you want this project, how your school will use this project and how it will benefit the students for years to come.

You and your team are now throwing the stone into the water. The long-term ripple effects are dependent on all of the thoughtful ground work you have completed as well as the details that you will be deciding.

*"When one tugs at a single thing in nature,
he finds it attached to the rest of the world."*

— *John Muir*

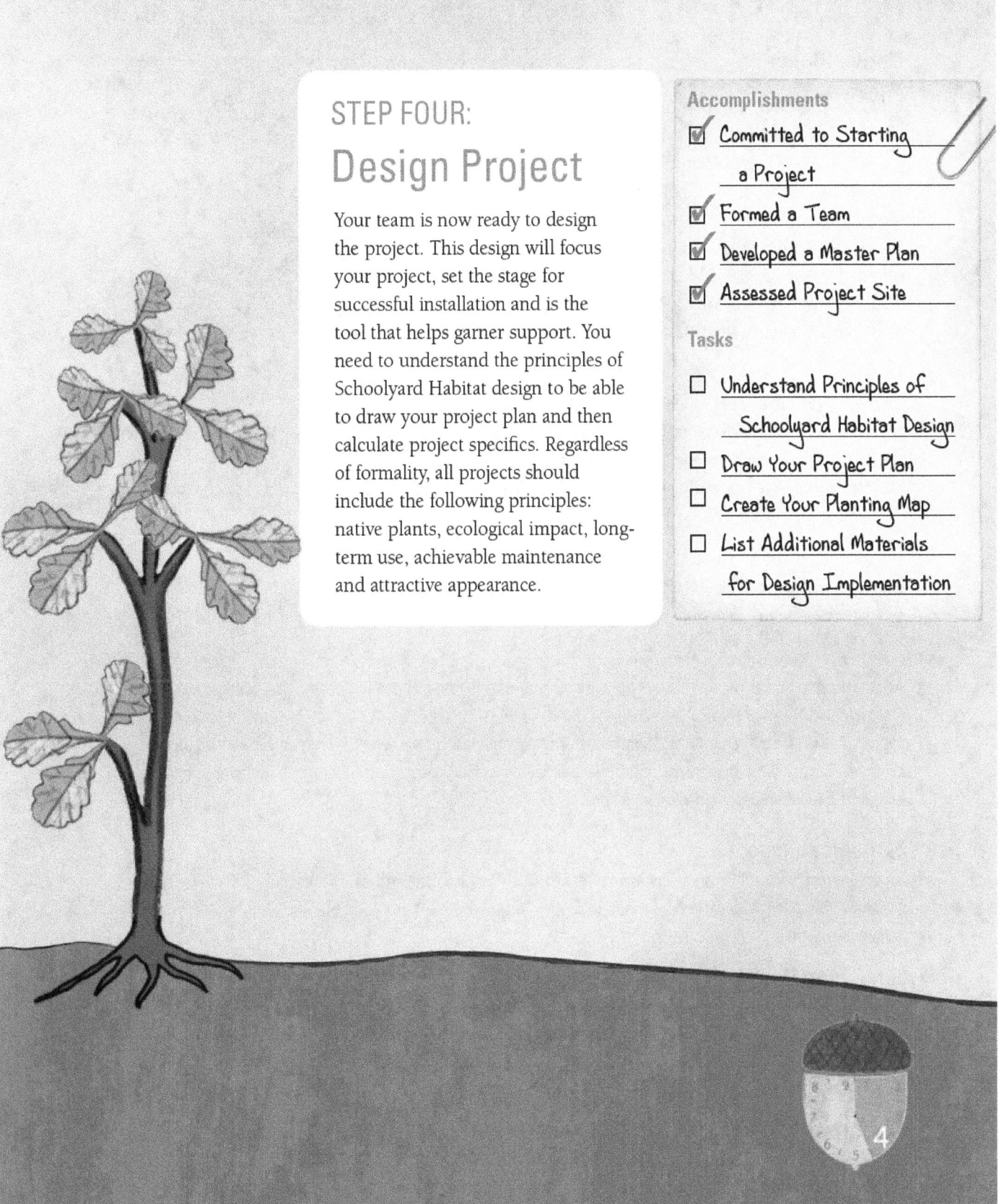

# STEP FOUR:
# Design Project

Your team is now ready to design the project. This design will focus your project, set the stage for successful installation and is the tool that helps garner support. You need to understand the principles of Schoolyard Habitat design to be able to draw your project plan and then calculate project specifics. Regardless of formality, all projects should include the following principles: native plants, ecological impact, long-term use, achievable maintenance and attractive appearance.

**Accomplishments**

☑ Committed to Starting a Project

☑ Formed a Team

☑ Developed a Master Plan

☑ Assessed Project Site

**Tasks**

☐ Understand Principles of Schoolyard Habitat Design

☐ Draw Your Project Plan

☐ Create Your Planting Map

☐ List Additional Materials for Design Implementation

4

# Understand Principles of Schoolyard Habitat Design

## Native Plants

### • What are native plants?

Native plants are those that evolved naturally in your region. They are adapted to local soils and climate conditions and generally require less watering and fertilizing than non-natives. Natives are often more resistant to insects and disease as well and, therefore, are less likely to need pesticides. Additionally, local and migratory wildlife have adapted to and are dependent upon native species for food, cover and rearing young. Using locally native plants helps preserve the balance and beauty of natural ecosystems.

*To find out what plants are native to your area, contact your state native plant society, county extension office or talk with the natural resource professional on your team.*

### • What are non-native plants?

Organisms are considered non-native (sometimes referred to as alien, exotic, foreign, introduced, non-indigenous) when they occur artificially in locations beyond their historical ranges. Non-native includes any species moved from one locality to another outside of the species' natural range.

### • What are invasive plants?

Invasive plants reproduce rapidly and establish themselves over a large area. This growth overwhelms and displaces existing native vegetation and forms dense single species stands.

### • Why do we care?

As non-native and invasive plants replace existing native ones, there is a lower diversity of native plants available to provide the necessary habitat needs for wildlife. While some animals have a varied diet and can feed on a wide number of plant species, many are highly specialized and are restricted to feeding on a select plant species. Using native plants helps keep the focus of your project on local wildlife and habitat issues.

## Ecological Impact

An ecologically sound project focuses on local watershed, habitat and wildlife issues. Therefore, your site should replicate historic or pre-settlement habitat to the extent possible and should be significant in size and scope.

## Long-Term Use

Your design should reflect the way that your school community intends to use the project. It should reflect how you imagine your students interacting with and learning from the habitat you create. A larger habitat supports a greater number of students who can immerse themselves within it. You should also consider the accessibility for disabled students and the length of time it will take for classes to walk to the habitat site.

## Achievable Maintenance

Your design should realistically reflect your teams' availability to take care of the habitat.

*More formal projects need greater maintenance. More naturalized projects need less maintenance.*

## Attractive Appearance

Understanding some of these basic landscape design concepts can help improve the appearance of any habitat, even a naturalized one.

Balance: Balance can be symmetrical creating a more formal landscape in which one side of an area mirrors the other. An informal or natural look is achieved through an asymmetrical balance such as placing a group of shrubs on one side of an area with a single tree on the other side.

Repetition: Arrange similar elements throughout a space by repeating forms, textures or curves. Repetition unifies your design. One way this can be achieved is by interspersing clumps of the same flowers throughout the habitat.

Contrast: Contrast creates variety in the landscape. To create contrasts, place plants with big leaves next to fine textures or one bright color next to another.

Color: Planting masses of color within the project can create a strong visual impact and help attract pollinator species.

*Mowed edges along natural areas create a clean border that make a space look orderly and purposeful. Designating the area with a sign also helps people understand that this natural area was by design.*

Shapes: Curves replicate nature better than straight lines. Curved lines fool your eyes to make spaces seem larger or more distinct. This is especially important when dealing with a small site. A small space looks more confined when its edges are obvious. Use shrubs or tall grasses to soften the straight lines of a fence or wall. Or use open fencing materials such as coyote fencing, split rail or lattice, to gently define a boundary.

# Draw Your Project Plan

You will use this drawing to calculate the quantity of plants and materials needed and provide to volunteers or paid contractors working on the project. This drawing will also be the basis for describing your project to others in the community. This plan in combination with your planting map will become your project design.

Have fun and be creative. You and your team have the knowledge, confidence and desire to create a truly fun and valuable Schoolyard Habitat. Use the information you have collected as well as the principles of design to create your drawing.

Refer to the appendices for specific design considerations for your habitat project. The information contained there is very important for completing your project design. In addition, contact 888-258-0808 for your local area's utility referral service to have someone come and mark the location of underground utilities! When drawing your design, account for any utilities that fall within your project site.

## Example of a Project Plan: Cityport Elementary School

*Most projects can use a student or teacher drawn design. In some cases, a professional design is required.*

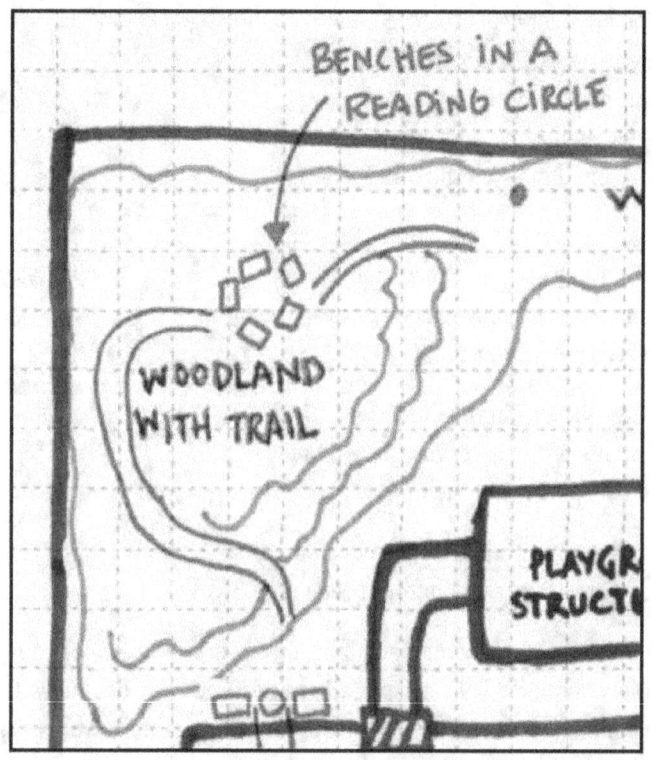

## Example of a Project Plan: Countryside High School

*A project such as this encompasses all of the design features and materials listed in this step.*

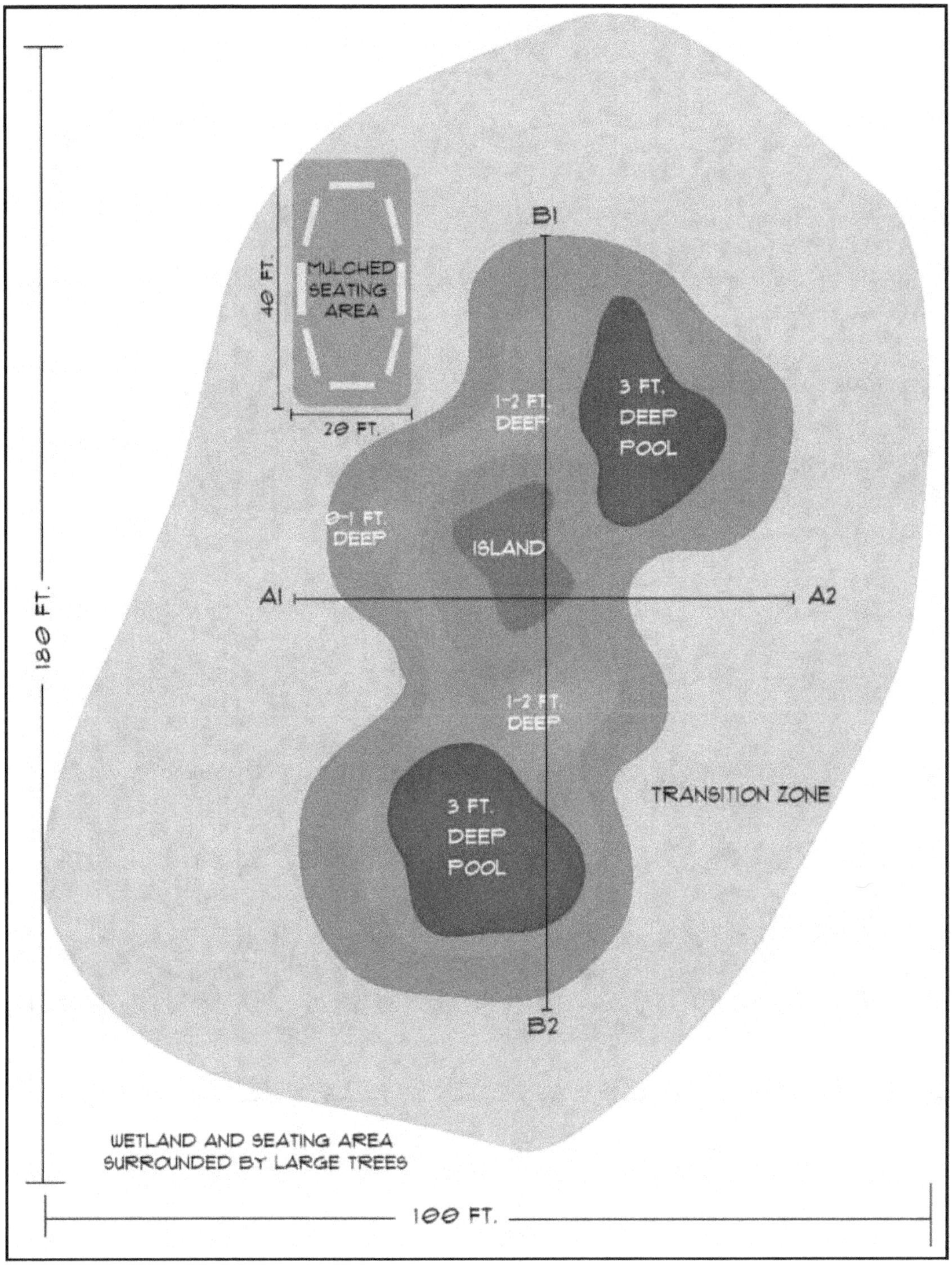

40 FT.

MULCHED
SEATING
AREA

20 FT.

B1

1-2 FT.
DEEP

3 FT.
DEEP
POOL

0-1 FT.
DEEP

ISLAND

A1

A2

180 FT.

1-2 FT.
DEEP

3 FT.
DEEP
POOL

TRANSITION ZONE

B2

WETLAND AND SEATING AREA
SURROUNDED BY LARGE TREES

100 FT.

## Example of a Project Plan Continued: Countryside High School

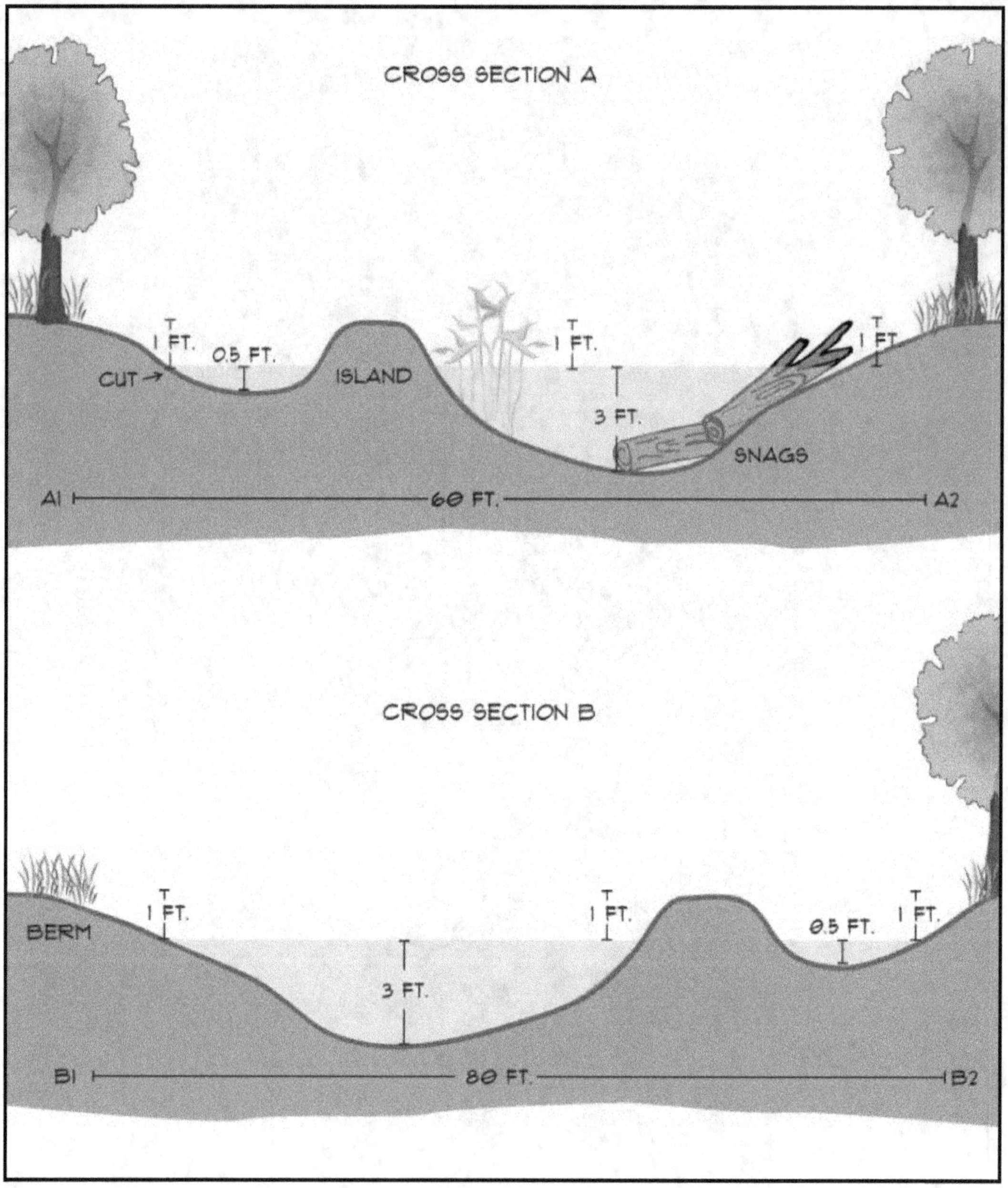

CROSS SECTION A

CUT →

1 FT.

0.5 FT.

ISLAND

1 FT.

3 FT.

1 FT.

SNAGS

A1 ——————————— 60 FT. ——————————— A2

CROSS SECTION B

BERM

1 FT.

3 FT.

1 FT.

0.5 FT.

1 FT.

B1 ——————————— 80 FT. ——————————— B2

# Field Notes for Drawing Your Project Plan

### Procedure:

1. Before leaving the classroom, review the project site assessment data and goals from Step 3 Assess Project Site.

2. Go to the area designated for the project.

3. Divide into teams of two or three. Draw a design for the site that includes all of the elements of your chosen project.

4. Measure size of specific features. For example, length and width of path or area designated for seating.

5. Write a phrase or two about each element of the design to support your ideas.

6. Have each group present its plan to the class.

7. As a group, decide what element of each plan you like.

8. Take these ideas and create a collaborative project plan.

*"Those who contemplate the beauty of the earth find reserves of strength that will endure as long as life lasts. There is symbolic as well as actual beauty in the migration of birds, the ebb and flow of the tides, the folded bud ready for the spring. There is something infinitely healing in the repeated refrains of nature- the assurance that dawn comes after night, and spring after the winter."*

— *Rachel Carson*

# Create Your Planting Map

First, research and create a list of native plants you will use in your habitat. Then, calculate the number of plants needed to cover your desired planting area. Finally, place your plants on a map.

## Considerations for choosing and mapping plant species

**Height:** Consider the mature size of the plant relative to the project and its position in the site.

**Sunlight:** Note shade tolerance when choosing plants and placement within the project.

**Color:** Choose plants that bloom when students are in session. Look for color combinations and contrasts to aesthetically accent your project throughout the seasons, particularly leaves during fall, bark in winter and flowers in spring.

**Wildlife value:** Choose plants to maintain a seasonal balance of habitat and attract a diversity of wildlife to your project.

**Rate of spread:** Place faster spreading plants further apart, slow spreading plants can be placed closer together to achieve desired cover.

**Education:** Choosing trees with different leaf shapes can help teach taxonomy. You may want to select plants Native Americans used for food and medicinal uses. Also, consider species that have a variety of seed types to study dispersal mechanisms or test germination methods.

**Biodiversity:** Develop a plant list that mimics a natural level of biodiversity and pattern. It is not possible to include every species in a guide and not every species is available at a local nursery.

Have the planting map reviewed by the natural resource professional on your team, by someone at your local university extension office or by the nursery where you purchase your plants.

## Calculate number of plants needed

Use the square footage of your habitat area and the formula below to calculate the number of plants needed. Generally, for naturalized plantings, calculate one flower or grass for every 2 sq ft and one tree or shrub for every 8 sq ft. The following formula can help determine the number of plants needed.

$$\frac{\text{Area to be planted in ft}^2}{(\text{Distance apart in ft})^2} = \frac{A}{D^2} = A \div D^2 = \text{Number of plants}$$

*D = 1.5 for slow spreading plants, 2 for medium spreading plants, 3 for fast spreaders and 8 for trees or shrubs.*

*"Birth, life, and death — each took place on the hidden side of a leaf."*

*— Toni Morrison*

# Field Notes for Choosing Your Plants

**Procedure:**

1. Gather native plant nursery catalogs, native plant books, field guides and regional website plant resources to provide a list of appropriate plants.
2. Split into small groups.
3. Choose plants using your resources as a guide.
4. Fill in the plant chart below. Use the notes column to describe why you have chosen each plant.
5. Have teams share their ideas with the whole class.
6. As a class, create a collaborative plant list.

|    | Scientific name | Common name | Notes |
|----|-----------------|-------------|-------|
| 1  |                 |             |       |
| 2  |                 |             |       |
| 3  |                 |             |       |
| 4  |                 |             |       |
| 5  |                 |             |       |
| 6  |                 |             |       |
| 7  |                 |             |       |
| 8  |                 |             |       |
| 9  |                 |             |       |
| 10 |                 |             |       |
| 11 |                 |             |       |
| 12 |                 |             |       |
| 13 |                 |             |       |
| 14 |                 |             |       |
| 15 |                 |             |       |

*"To exist as a nation, to prosper as a state, and to live as a people, we must have trees."*

— *Theodore Roosevelt*

*Examples of planting maps for Cityport Elementary School and Countryside High School.*

## Example of a Planting Map: Cityport Elementary School

```
⋰ = FLOWER        = SMALL       T = TREE
    SEEDS           SHRUBS
    THROUGHOUT
```

├── 100 FEET ──┤

SEED MIXTURE TO
INCLUDE:
- NARROW LEAF
  MILKWEED
- STICKY MONKEY
  FLOWER
- CALIFORNIA FUSIA
- WESTERN CONEFLOWER
- DEER GRASS
- PURPLE NEEDLE GRASS

T   T   T   T   T   T
T   T   T
T   T
T   T
├─ 20 FT. ─┤
20 FT.   BENCHES & MULCH
T   T
T   T

FLOWER BEDS

STREET        50 FEET

22 TREES:
- LIVE OAK
- SYCAMORE
- WESTERN REDBUD

T   T
T   T
T

36 SHRUBS:
- COYOTE BUSH
- ELDERBERRY
- CEANOTHUS

T   T   T
T

← EACH FLOWER BED IS
  APPROX. 30 SQUARE FEET

TRAIL

FLOWER BEDS

SCHOOL BUILDING

WALKWAY IS APPROX. 250 FT. LONG AND 3 FT. WIDE

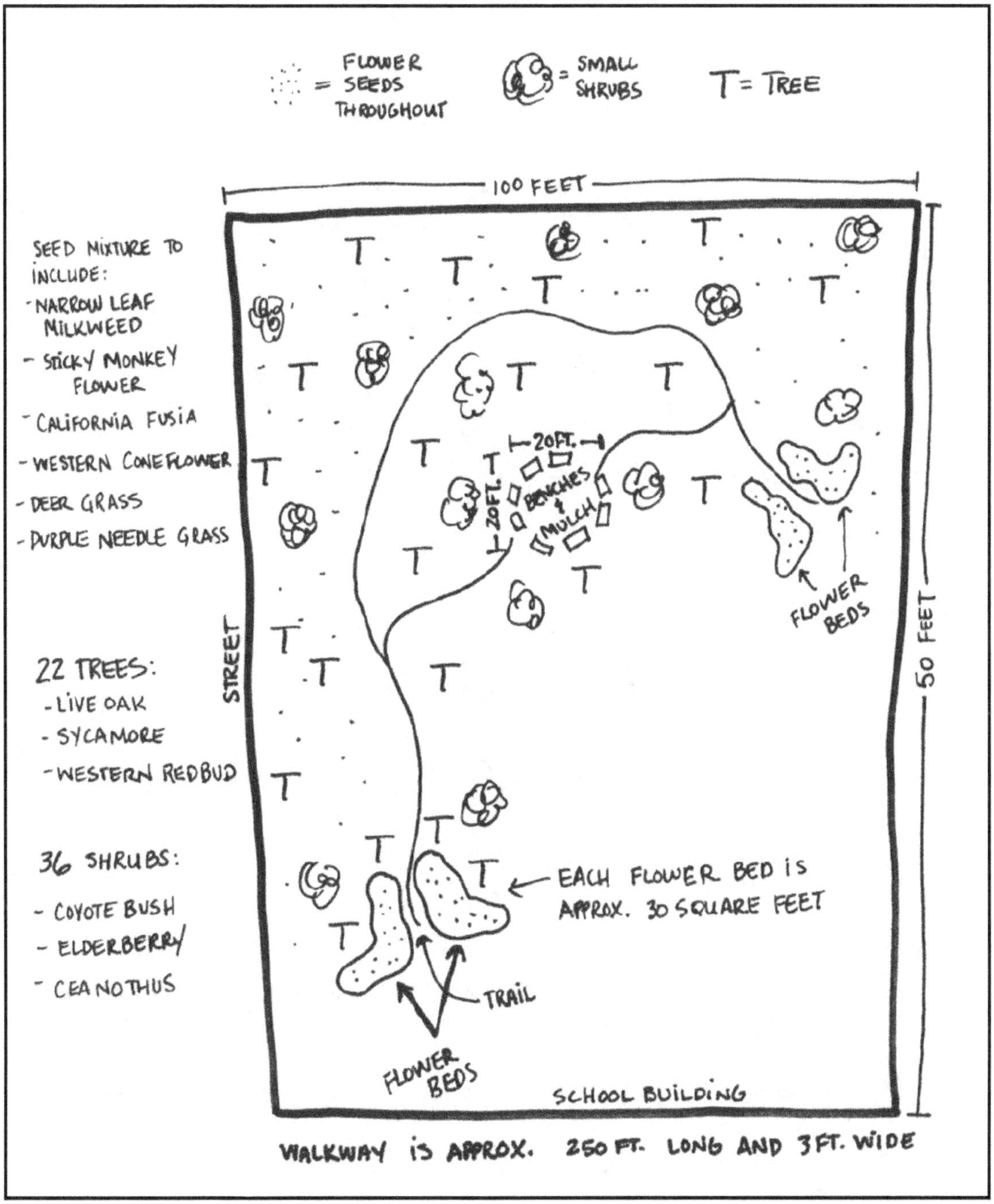

## Example of a Planting Map: Countryside High School

COUNTRYSIDE HIGH SCHOOL PLANTING MAP
TOTAL AREA = 18,000 SQUARE FEET

MULCHED SEATING AREA

40 FT.

20 FT.

DEEP POOL

ISLAND

180 FT.

DEEP POOL

TRANSITION ZONE

100 FT.

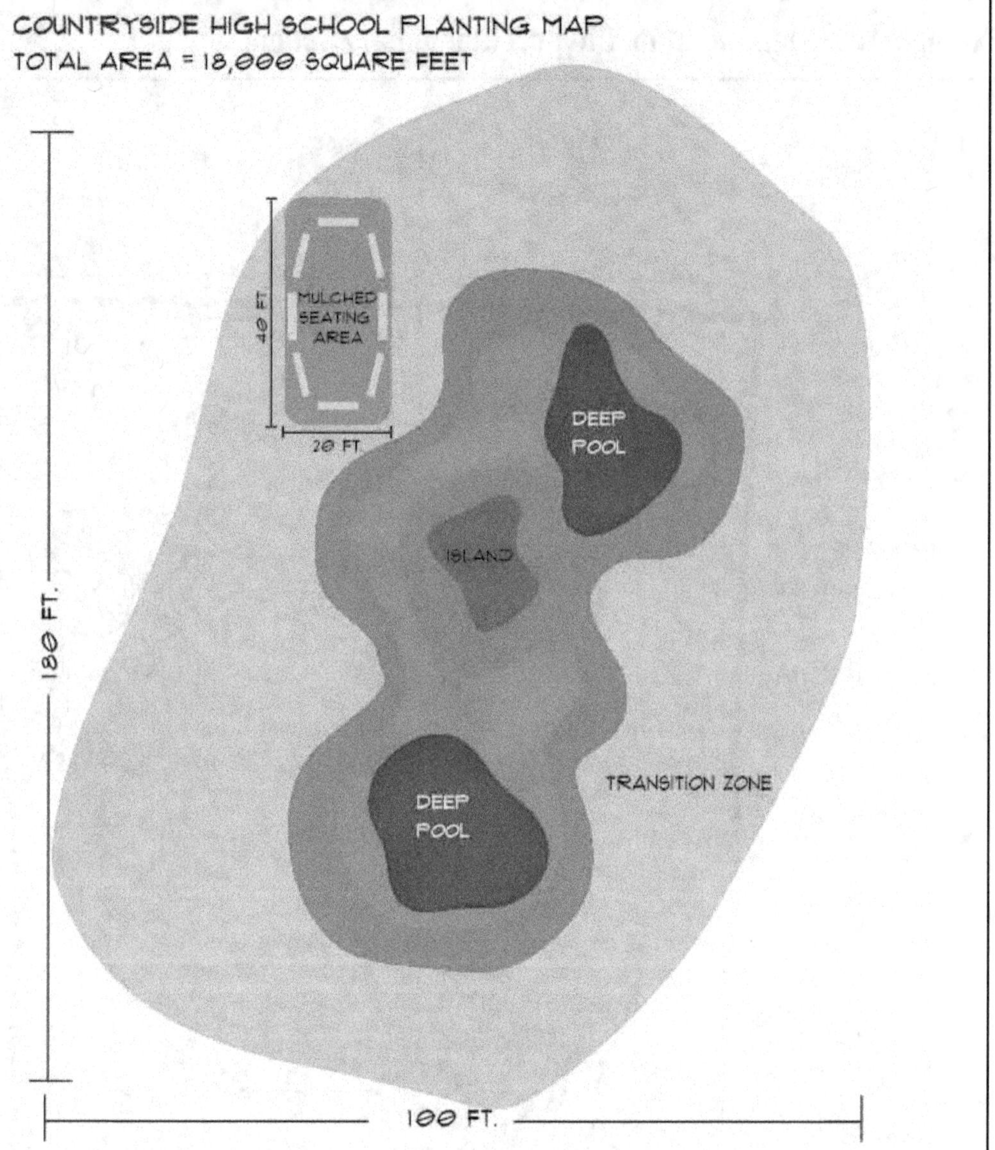

**Transition Zone:** Approx. 8,000 sq. ft. – 38 trees and shrubs and 15 lbs. of seeds of the following species: swamp white oak, river birch, monkey flower, cardinal flower, marsh hibiscus, sweetspire, green bulrush, switchgrass

**0 to 1 foot deep:** Approx. 4,000 sq. ft. – 2,000 plants total of the following species: soft rush, pickerelweed, three-square

**1 to 2 foot deep:** Approx. 4,000 sq. ft. – 2,000 plants total of the following species: arrow arum, spatterdock

**3 foot deep pool:** Approx. 1,200 sq. ft. – open water, no plants

# Field Notes for Creating Planting Map

**Procedure:**

1. Use the drawing of your project plan, plant list and the plant quantities calculated to illustrate where the plants will be planted. If possible, draw your planting map directly onto a copy of your project plan.

2. Set up a mock planting at the project site. Use various materials or containers to represent the plants. Is your team satisfied with your map?
   If not, update your map to reflect your desired result.

3. Combine or overlay your planting map with your project plan to create a complete project design.

*"Eventually we'll realize that if we destroy the ecosystem, we destroy ourselves."*

*— Jonas Salk*

# List Additional Materials for Design Implementation

In Step 5, you will be creating your budget. In order to do this, you need to list all of the materials and supplies called for in your project design. Below is a list of common materials needed. It is preferable to have a few too many materials than not enough.

## Tools and Supplies

Consider all the materials you need for project installation as well as the continued use of the habitat. This includes shovels and tools, materials for benches and paths, as well as clipboards and materials for educational use.

### Countryside High School supply list:

☐ Project design

☐ Permanent markers, cards and tape to label plants

☐ Work gloves

☐ Buckets

☐ Stakes and flags

☐ Shovels and trowels

☐ Garden sheers or clippers

☐ Rakes

☐ Pick axes

☐ Wheelbarrows

☐ Mechanical tiller

☐ Hoses and water key

☐ Timer for watering system

☐ Mulch

☐ Clipboards

☐ Drinking water and snacks

☐ Trash bags

☐ First aid kits

☐ Cameras and binoculars

*Countryside High School checklist for planting day includes materials and supplies needed for their project installation and use.*

## Soil amendments

Some sites have been altered to the point that they no longer support the diversity of native plants you would like to have. With the help of the natural resource professional on the team, use the soil information from the project site assessment in Step 3 to determine if any soil amendments are needed. Common amendments include compost and fish emulsion.

## Excavation

If your project design calls for any earth moving, you will need to acquire necessary permits. Know the type of equipment you are going to use as well as where the soil will go. Small projects may be able to use the soil in another location on site, while larger projects may need to pay for removal. In either case, you will need to use special equipment. Refer to Appendix E for more details on commonly used equipment. The maintenance personnel or natural resource professional on your team will help guide you through this more technical aspect of your project design.

## Mulch

**Uses:** Mulch has many beneficial uses. It reduces weeds, prevents water loss, regulates soil temperature and provides a distinct border. To have these benefits, mulch should be applied 2 to 4 inches thick.

**Types:** Types of mulch include, wood chips, bark, fallen leaves, rocks and ½ inch or smaller gravel.

**Sources:** Many city and county facilities as well as public utilities offer free mulch. However, make sure any mulch you are getting is free from trash and harmful plants and has been composted to eliminate any weed seeds. Generally, rock materials need to be purchased and should be included in your budget.

Frank Marsden

*Keep in mind that many native pollinator bees nest underground. Leave an unmulched area to provide adequate habitat for these native pollinators.*

## Calculating quantities of soil and mulch

Soil and mulch volumes are referred to in cubic yards (yd³), where 1 yd³ = 27 cubic feet (ft³). They can be ordered in bulk by the cubic yard or in bags containing 2 or 3 cubic feet. Be aware of these units as you measure and complete your order.

You will need to store soil and mulch if delivered prior to project installation. Find an approved and protected place to store these materials before use.

### Formula:

First: calculate depth in feet, then calculate quantities of mulch or soil.

(planting area in ft² x depth of mulch in feet*) ÷ 27 ft³/yd³ = yd³

*Be sure to convert inches to feet for all of your calculations where the number of inches divided by 12 equals the number of feet.*

### Examples:

A layer of mulch 3 inches deep over a project area of 1,000 ft² would require 250 ft³ or 9.25 yd³ of mulch.

3 inches deep = 3 in ÷ 12 in per ft = 0.25 ft
(1,000 ft² x 0.25 ft) ÷ 27 ft3/yd³ = 9.25 yd³ of mulch

A hole 18 inches deep with an area of 2,400 ft² would require 133 yd³ of soil removed
18 inches deep = 18 in ÷ 12 in per ft = 1.5 ft
(2,400 ft² x 1.5 ft) ÷ 27 ft3/yd³ = 133 yd³ of soil removed

3 ways to order 1 yd³ of mulch

- or - - or -

Nine
3-cubic-foot bags

Fourteen
2-cubic-foot bags

Pickup truck full of 1-cubic-yard

# STEP FIVE:
## Decide Money Matters

You and your team must create a detailed budget. The budget identifies both the amount of funding necessary to complete the project and resources already available. To develop a budget, you need to have a list of needs and resources. Determine what resources you already have and decide how you will acquire the remaining, cash, materials and labor.

### Accomplishments
- ☑ Committed to Starting a Project
- ☑ Formed a Team
- ☑ Developed a Master Plan
- ☑ Assessed Project Site
- ☑ Designed Project

### Tasks
- ☐ Develop a List of Needs and Resources
- ☐ Craft a Budget
- ☐ Acquire Resources

5

*"True wisdom consists in not departing from nature and in molding our conduct according to her laws and model."*

— *Seneca*

# Develop a List of Needs and Resources

## Needs

Build on your existing lists and create a comprehensive one of everything your project requires. Attach an estimated cost to each item on the list. To get an accurate account of how much some services and materials will cost, call and get estimates, go to stores, or do online searches. Decide if you will be creating a budget for your entire master plan or for individual phases. Look ahead to the steps that follow the budget. It is critical to consider the entire cost of installing, maintaining and using the project now. Putting this information into a simple chart will give you an at-a-glance budget and help organize a strategy for funding the project.

## Resources

Now that you have accounted for all your needs, determine the value of the resources you already have. For example, the school may have tools and materials leftover from past projects or parents may have already volunteered to help. Remember, time is money, so time should be accounted for. The value associated with items that are free or discounted will be needed when acquiring funding. Use the budget examples provided here to help you with this process.

*This table lists project needs and matches them to existing resources. This can help determine what your remaining needs are and how to move forward to fill those gaps.*

**PROJECT NEEDS**
(Materials and Labor)

- Curriculum activities for teachers
- Project design
- 500 native plant plugs
- Snacks for planting day
- First aid kits
- Bird box materials
- Decomposed granite for trail
- 125 Gallon sized trees
- Excavation of wetland
- Tools for planting
- 20 Clipboards for students
- Tool storage
- Flagging for staging plants
- 300' of hose
- Maintenance for first year

**EXISTING RESOURCES**
(Supplies, People and Organizations)

- Local native nursery
- Construction assistance from Rock Creek Watershed Association
- Cityport school beautification fund
- Cityport Creek PTA
- School district maintenance tool shed
- Local store
- Local hardware store
- Students

# Craft a Budget

Creating a simple budget, even if not seeking outside support, will allow you to show administrators and other project supporters that you have carefully thought through this process and reassure them that building the project is feasible. When your needs exceed your resources, your budget is a tool to help you fill those needs.

As your budget becomes more detailed and funds are realized, you will make more complex decisions about project implementation. For example, if you have ample funding for plants you may choose larger plants to start, or if your cash flow is small you may choose plug sized plants instead of quarts.

*These budgets show examples of projects and costs with increasing complexity.*

## Simple budget where no outside funds are needed.

| Item | Unit Cost | # of units | Shipping | In-kind | Total |
|---|---|---|---|---|---|
| Trees | $10 | 22 | $30.00 | | $250 |
| Wildflower quarts | $2 | 40 | | 10% | $72 |
| Benches | $50 | 8 | | | $400 |
| Stepping stones | $8 | 20 | | 10% | $144 |
| Asphalt removal | $5,000 | 1 | | $5,000 | $5,000 |
| Soil addition | $40 | 5 yards | | | $200 |
| Mulch | $30 | 10 yards | | $300 | $300 |
| Hoses | $50 | 2 | | | $100 |
| Soil removal | $500 | 1 | | | $500 |
| Habitat plant books | $5 | 4 | | | $20 |
| Habitat sign | $15 | 1 | | | $15 |
| **TOTAL** | | | | | **$7,001** |
| **EXISTING FUNDS** | | | | | **$7,001** |

## A more detailed budget showing outside funds received.

| Item | Total Cost | Grant Award | Cash Match | In-kind Match | Source of Match |
|---|---|---|---|---|---|
| Native Plants | $778.50 | $700.65 | --- | $77.85 | Nursery discount |
| Excavation | $500.00 | | $500.00 | | PTA |
| Soil amendments | $158.34 | $158.34 | --- | --- | --- |
| Hoses, nozzles, etc. | $60.86 | $60.86 | --- | --- | --- |
| Plant tags | $18.45 | $18.45 | --- | --- | --- |
| Mileage – 90 miles x $.505 per mile x 6 trips | $272.70 | $272.70 | --- | --- | --- |
| **TOTAL** | **$1788.85** | **$1211.00** | **$500.00** | **$77.85** | --- |

**Complex budget including materials for multiple phases.**

| BUDGET FOR COUNTRYSIDE HIGH SCHOOL HABITAT RESTORATION | | | | | | | |
|---|---|---|---|---|---|---|---|
| **Phase 1: Wetland      Phase 2: Seating** | | | | | **Revenue Sources** | | |
| Item/Service | Cost/Unit | Unit | Quantity | Total Cost | Grant | Donations | Existing and In-kind Resources |
| **SITE PREPARATION** | | | | | | | |
| Excavation | $1900.00 | 1 | 1 | $1,900.00 | $1,900.00 | | |
| Herbicide | $986.00 | 2.5gal | 1 | $986.00 | $ 986.00 | | |
| **INSTALLATION MATERIALS** | | | | | | | |
| **PLANTS** | | | | | | | |
| Native plants – trees and shrubs | $15.00 | ea | 38 | $570 .00 | $570.00 | | |
| Native plants – herbaceous wetland quarts | $2.00 | ea | 90 | $270.00 | $270.00 | | |
| Native plants – herbaceous wetland plugs | $0.75 | ea | 1,000 | $750.00 | $750.00 | | |
| Native grass seed | $15.00 | lb | 30 | $450.00 | $450.00 | | |
| Native plant delivery | $140.00 | 1 | 1 | $140.00 | | $140.00 | |
| **IRRIGATION** | | | | | | | |
| Irrigation line 3/4" 1000 ft roll | $90.00 | roll | 2 | $180.00 | $180.00 | | |
| Irrigation line 500 ft roll | $50.00 | roll | 1 | $50.00 | $50.00 | | |
| Emitters 1 gal/hour | $0.55 | ea | 200 | $110.00 | $110.00 | | |
| Irrigation stakes | $14.00 | 100pk | 2 | $28.00 | $28.00 | | |
| Pokers | $0.49 | ea | 10 | $4.90 | $4.90 | | |
| Cutters | $8.75 | ea | 5 | $43.75 | $43.75 | | |
| Connectors - in line, T's, figure 8 | $30.00 | lump | 1 | $30.00 | $30.00 | | |
| Timer | $40.00 | ea | 1 | $40.00 | $40.00 | | |
| **FEATURES** | | | | | | | |
| Materials for benches | $100.00 | ea | 6 | $600.00 | $600.00 | | |
| Mulch | $25.00 | yard | 15 | $375.00 | | $375.00 | |
| Owl box - box, post, hardware | $125.00 | ea | 1 | $125.00 | $125.00 | | |
| **TOOLS** | | | | | | | |
| Shovels | $25.00 | ea | 15 | $375.00 | | | $375.00 |
| Gloves | $6.00 | ea pair | 30 | $180.00 | $180.00 | | |
| Hoes | $20.00 | ea | 10 | $200.00 | $200.00 | | |
| Field flags | $12.00 | 100pk | 2 | $24.00 | $24.00 | | |
| **INSTALLATION LABOR** | | | | | | | |
| Student workers | $8.00 | hour | 150 | $1,200.00 | | | $1,200.00 |
| Volunteer workers | $15.00 | hour | 100 | $1,500.00 | | | $1,500.00 |
| **EDUCATIONAL MATERIALS** | | | | | | | |
| Native plant field guides | $15.00 | ea | 10 | $150.00 | | $150.00 | |
| Binoculars | $20.00 | ea | 15 | $300.00 | $300.00 | | |
| **TOTAL PROJECT COSTS** | | | | **$10581.65** | **$6841.65** | **$665.00** | **$ 3075.00** |

# Acquire Resources

Your detailed budget is the tool to help you secure your unmet needs. There are three levels of community that can help you achieve your financial goals. It is best to start locally and move beyond each level as necessary.

• School community: fundraising and donations

• Local community: donations and grants

• Outside local community: grants

There are many types of items you can ask for and many ways of raising funds. The more personal and local you can make the effort, the higher the likelihood your project will receive the resources it needs.

| PROJECT NEEDS (Materials and Labor) | EXISTING RESOURCES (Supplies, People and Organizations) |
|---|---|
| Curriculum activities for teachers | Federal grant |
| Project design | Parent business donation |
| 500 native plant plugs | Federal grant |
| Snacks for planting day | Penny drive |
| First aid kits | Penny drive |
| Bird box materials | Parent business donation |
| 125 Gallon sized trees | Local native nursery |
| Decomposed granite for trail | Construction assistance from Rock Creek Watershed Association |
| Excavation of wetland | |
| Tools for planting | Cityport school beautification fund |
| 20 Clipboards for students | Cityport PTA |
| Tool storage | School district maintenance tool shed |
| Flagging for staging plants | Local store |
| 300' of hose | Local hardware store |
| Maintenance for first year | Students |

## Fundraising

Fundraising activities provide a way to generate local cash contributions. Think creatively and outside of the usual schools fundraisers, and the possibilities are endless.

Pros: Allows for control over who, what, when, where and how much

Cons: Requires a lot of effort and many small steps to achieve larger goal

Fundraising is a great way to support your project, involve many students, partner with your school community and create small successes. If fundraising is a significant activity required to support the project, a phased approach to implementation is best. A sequence of successes often sparks more interest and therefore more partners to support the project through donations of money, equipment, supplies or time. Fundraisers can include bake sales, car washes, recycling collection, dinners, ice cream socials, service projects and raffles. You should start with these smaller, more local efforts as early as possible to demonstrate to grantors and local businesses that there is a lot of school support for your project. Fundraising can also be done on a larger scale by asking local businesses to become a sponsor, perhaps by placing a fundraising jar at their business or through donation of goods or services to an auction.

## Donations

Donations are gifts received in the form of cash, materials or labor. Be specific about your needs. Do not take items that are not wanted or stray from project goals based on the donations.

**Pros:** Costly labor or expensive materials can be discounted or free

**Cons:** May not be exactly what you are expecting or need, donations of labor are often over-promised and under-delivered

Donations are sometimes referred to as in-kind donations which means, donated goods or services. Soliciting for donations provides an excellent opportunity for students to write formal letters to people, businesses and organizations in their local community. Not only will people in the community learn about your students, they will learn about the project at the school.

Donation requests can be formal or informal. Researching the businesses and organizations you are soliciting will help you or your students find a donor with a mission that closely matches your need. Let a potential donor know upfront the kind of publicity that you can provide in return for his or her support.

### Potential places to look for funding or donations:

- Local businesses and corporations
- Local natural resource or parks offices
- Local construction or landscaping companies
- Garden clubs
- Native plant societies
- Scout groups

- Local universities
- State and county extension offices
- High school and college service groups
- Local media
- Parent teacher organizations
- Environmental and civic organizations

## Sample Donation Letter

December 22, 2010

Mr. Jeffrey Johnson
149 Maple Lane
Countryside, MD 11111

Dear Mr. Johnson,

I am writing to you on behalf of the Countryside High School Schoolyard Habitat Team. The Countryside High School Schoolyard Habitat Team is an afterschool club dedicated to creating a habitat for wildlife and an outdoor classroom for our whole school to enjoy. Our objective is to raise awareness about our local watershed, while protecting wildlife, and raise funds to build an extraordinary place on our campus. We are currently requesting donations of cash, materials and labor to help us with our project. The first phase of our habitat will include 36 native trees, a 4,800 sq ft wetland and an open space for quiet study that will include several benches our shop class is building.

| Donations we have received | Donations still needed |
|---|---|
| $500 – Schools Credit Union | Sod cutter rental |
| 20 trowels – Ron's Hardware | 3 cubic yards organic mulch |
| 3 volunteer hours from 3 PTA members | 20 volunteer hours |

As students, we are dedicating our time, energy and enthusiasm to work for this cause. Given that most of us live in the community, we request your support by considering a donation. It could be in the form of gift certificates for products or services available at your facility.

We are preparing a groundbreaking celebration on September 9, 2011 and would like to invite everyone who has helped us achieve our goal. In return for your generosity, the name of your company will appear on our posters, banners, advertisements and brochure.

Thank you for considering our request. If you have any questions or need further information, please feel free to contact one of our team members. I will follow up with a phone call in the next couple of days.

If you decide to contribute, please send your donation to:
Countryside High School Schoolyard Habitat Team
149 Maple Lane
Countryside, MD 11111

Sincerely,
Julie Denny
123-123-5555

## Grants

Grants are formal request for funding from agencies, organizations and businesses with giving programs. Before your team applies for a grant be sure to inform your administrators.

**Pros:** Grants are usually large cash amounts, very specific in what they will fund and have clear guidelines for their applications

**Cons:** They are not guaranteed and decisions for funding may not be in sync with your project timeline

Many organizations offer grant funding for Schoolyard Habitat projects. There is increasing competition for these grants. Identify potential grantors by searching online, or by contacting the foundation center and your state environmental education association. Call the office of the granting organization you are applying to before writing and submitting your grant. Talk to the grant manager to assess if your project matches their priorities. Include student work in your grant application to show grant reviewers how involved the students are and add a personal touch to your application. If possible, invite the grantor to the project site to get feedback and show off your well designed plan. If it does not fit their criteria, they may know of a grant that does.

| Year One | Year Two | Year Three | Ongoing |
|---|---|---|---|
| | Plants | Weather Station | Habitat |
| | Mulch | Bird and Bat Boxes | Weather Station |
| | Field Guides | Habitat | Bird and Bat Boxes |
| Plants | Benches | Benches | Benches |
| Mulch | Habitat | Field Guides | Field Guides |
| Tools | Tools | Tools | Tools |
| Curricular Resources | Curricular Resources | Curricular Resources | Curricular Resources |
| Master Plan | Master Plan | Master Plan | Master Plan |

Existing Resources    Fundraising    Donations    Grants

*Fundraising, grant writing and donations all cumulatively build on your existing resources to create the long term implementation of your schoolyard habitat master plan.*

# STEP SIX:
## Install Project

You have finally reached the step you have been working so hard to get to. Proper preparation of the ground, people and plants is essential. While there are many things to get accomplished in this section, don't get bogged down by the details and remember to involve the students as much as possible and have fun.

**Accomplishments**

- ☑ Committed to Starting a Project
- ☑ Formed a Team
- ☑ Developed a Master Plan
- ☑ Assessed Project Site
- ☑ Designed Project
- ☑ Decided Money Matters

**Tasks**

- ☐ Prepare the Site
- ☐ Prepare the People
- ☐ Create a Work Plan
- ☐ Gather Materials and Supplies
- ☐ Plant Your Project

6

## Timing is Everything

It is helpful to create a timeline specific to project implementation such as the one below. Many of the tasks associated with project installation are unique to your specific project, use this sample as a guideline to create your own.

| | | At Least 1 Year Before | At Least 6 Months Before | At Least 1 Month Before | 1 Week Before | | For the Life of the Project |
|---|---|---|---|---|---|---|---|
| **STEP 6** | **PREPARE THE SITE** | Secure any Needed Permits<br><br>Secure any Needed Herbicide Applications | | | Finish any Excavation, Sod Removal or Auger Work | | |
| | **PREPARE THE PEOPLE** | | Schedule Date and Rain Date<br><br>Determine Number of Needed Volunteers | Create Planting Day Schedule | | **Planting Day** | Use, Monitor & Maintain Project |
| | **GATHER MATERIALS** | Find Growers of Native Plants | Reserve Nursery Order | Schedule Delivery | Have Plants Delivered – Keep Them Cool & Watered | | WATER! |

# Prepare the Site

Undoubtedly, there is something in the space where you would like to install your project, anything from sod to hard compacted soil, or even a structure or asphalt. Good ground preparation reduces future maintenance concerns. Presented here are the most common approaches to preparing your site. Your natural resource professional and maintenance team members will help you decide your approach.

The three stages of site preparation are as follows: remove unwanted plants, complete excavation and add soil amendments.

## A. Remove unwanted plants.

Unwanted plants include sod, non-native invasives and other plants that will inhibit the success of your project. Without complete removal, they will become a routine maintenance problem. Invasive plants can take over a project site before your native plants become established. You will find more information on managing invasive species in Step 7. Most commonly, you will need to remove sod from your project site.

## B. Complete any needed excavation or feature installation.

This can include, delineating a trail or path, removing asphalt, compacting an area for a pavilion or gazebo or digging a depression for a wetland. Complete this work at least a few days in advance of the planting. Alteration of existing irrigation lines should be done during the site preparation and excavation phase under the supervision of maintenance personnel from the school. It is required by law to call 888-258-0808 for your local area's utility referral service to come have utilities marked!

Many project features could potentially damage newly installed plants. It is important to install features in the correct order. For example, gazebos, trails, fences, signs, platforms, wildlife blinds, benches and large natural features like snags, brush piles and rocks should be placed before planting.

## C. Add soil amendments if needed.

Generally, for restoration projects using seedling and seed amendments are not needed. However, when working with containerized plants, it can help to mix some compost into the soil. Consult with your natural resource professional to determine any soil amendment needs for your specific site. Be sure to have soil amendments delivered before planting day and placed in a location that is easily accessible but does not interfere with project planting.

## Keep it Clean

When doing any type of soil disturbance it is necessary to protect local waterways from soil erosion by putting protection in place. This can come in the form of sediment erosion control fabric, straw bales or leaving strips of grass to collect sediment.

## Techniques for Sod Removal

There are a number of different ways to remove sod. The techniques that yield quick results can require considerable effort, while less labor intensive techniques may take at least a season to produce results. Listed below are four techniques for turning well established turf into an area ready for planting. Be sure to protect any nearby drains from sediment run-off in the event that there is rain between ground preparation and planting.

---

**Dig: This technique should be done the same week as planting.**

Digging is preparing the site by physically removing the layer of sod with a spade, shovel or sod cutter. This technique allows you to plant your site immediately.

Pros: Allows for immediate planting, avoids use of chemicals

Cons: Is labor intensive, exposes subsoil to weed seeds, removes organic matter, produces a lot of cumbersome waste sod material

- To dig up the sod, water the area a few days ahead of time to make the soil easier to work. The soil should be moist but not soggy. Saturated soil is not only heavy but also susceptible to compaction, which leads to poor plant growth.

- Cut the sod into parallel strips 1 foot wide using an edger or sharp spade. These strips can then be cut into 1 to 2 foot lengths, depending on the density of the turf and the thickness of the pieces. Next, pry up one end of a piece of sod and slide the spade or fork under it. Cut through any deep taproots, and lift out the precut piece, making sure to include the grass's fibrous roots.

- If you are installing a large project, consider renting a sod cutter. These steel-bladed, plow-like tools are more efficient than spades for large jobs, and they come in human- and gas-powered models.

- If the sod is in good condition, parents or volunteers may be willing to remove it from the site for reuse elsewhere. Otherwise, you will have to find other ways to dispose of it. Once the sod is gone, remove any rocks, remaining clumps of grass and sizable roots to make planting easier.

**Solarize: This technique should be started one growing season prior to planting.**

Solarizing uses plastic, newspaper or cardboard to kill the sod. This technique increases the temperature and blocks the light which eventually kills the sod. Students can be involved by bringing in materials from home and laying them down on the site. Regardless of what material you use to smother your site, water it prior to covering to ensure the process of decomposition takes place.

Pros: Retains and builds organic matter, does not disrupt soil structure, does not require the physical effort of removing or turning under sod

Cons: Delays planting up to several months, may kill beneficial organisms if using plastic

USFWS

- If using plastic to solarize, it can be covered for aesthetic purposes, but it isn't biodegradable and should eventually be removed.

- Cardboard and newspaper are great biodegradable alternatives. Lay down a thickness of six to eight sheets of newspaper at a minimum. Cover these biodegradable materials with grass clippings, leaves, mulch, or compost to hold the layers in place, keep in moisture, and add organic matter. Newspaper and cardboard do not increase temperature as much as plastic, but they eliminate light, causing chlorophyll to break down.

**Till: This technique should be started two months before planting.**

Tilling turns and mixes well established plants and roots until they are no longer living. This is not an appropriate technique for steep, erosion prone sites.

Pros: Retains and builds organic matter, machines do most of the work

Cons: Is difficult on rocky sites and in wet or clay soils, exposes and encourages certain weed seeds, repeated tilling may be detrimental to the soil structure

- Using a machine, till the top 2 inches of the soil. After tilling, allow any exposed seeds a few weeks to germinate, then either till again or spray with herbicide.

- Small tillers can usually handle previously worked soil, but breaking up well established sod or heavily compacted soil requires a heavier, rear tine unit and may require more than one pass. If your site is over 3,000 sq ft a larger machine should be used.

- After tilling the planting area, when feasible, rake and shape the soil to enhance the visual appeal of the site.

**Apply herbicides: This technique should be started two or more months prior to planting.**

Herbicides are chemicals that are sprayed onto plants to chemically stop the photosynthesis process. Check with your maintenance personnel, may or may not be an acceptable practice at your school and a licensed applicator may be required. Sometimes a letter home to parents and an amendment to the school's integrated pest management plan is all you need to move forward.

Pros: Is relatively simple and quick for those experienced in herbicide use, makes it easier to remove or turn grass, proven to be very effective for large areas

Cons: Risks injuring or killing nearby plants, can result in environmental contamination, personal injury or harm to beneficial organisms when used improperly.

• Choose an appropriate product. Be sure to buy a product designed to kill the dominant plant type covering your site.

• Follow label directions carefully. Use only products specifically formulated for the types of plants you want to kill. Glyphosate is a commonly used chemical for this practice. It is commonly sold in farm and garden stores.

• Don't apply herbicides when rain is expected, or the herbicide may wash off plants and into the soil and nearby waterways. Also, avoid applying on windy days to prevent drift onto nearby plantings. Wear protective clothing, such as gloves, long sleeves, long pants and a mask, when applying herbicides.

• Well established turf will require more than one application. It takes several days for effective absorption of herbicides. Grass and weed seeds in the soil will not be affected and may germinate later. After the first application, allow time for a second growth spurt to occur and complete the second application.

# Prepare the People

The better organized and trained the teams of students, teachers and volunteers are ahead of time the more smoothly the planting days will go. Installing the project requires the hard work of many helpers that could include multiple classes, the entire school or even multiple schools and the larger community.

Julie Dieguez

## Volunteers

Not all volunteers are accustomed to planting or are even comfortable working in the outdoors. Some are there simply to support their child's project. Alternately, some volunteers have a great deal of enthusiasm and love for planting and have a hard time letting the students do the work. It may be necessary to have a pre-planting day workshop to provide clear guidance to teachers, students and volunteers on how to properly plant plants and to go over the how-to and logistics of the day, so you can be confident things will go smoothly. It is important that all volunteers and team leaders become familiar with the planting plan before planting day.

## Students

All students, not only those that were involved in the design but also the entire student body are excited to be involved in the planting. Set expectations for spending time working on the project outside. Be sure they are prepared for the weather, wear appropriate shoes and clothes and understand why they are there. The value of the project will greatly increase if they know the benefits for both themselves and wildlife.

# Create a Work Plan

The work plan will guide activities on planting day. The exact amount of time that it takes to plant your project depends entirely on the size and scope of the project. Your work plan should include a schedule of activities for the day with assigned task lists for all involved, including students, teachers and volunteers.

• Review your project design and decide how many students your core team wants to participate and from which classes they will come.

## Alert the Media

Planting day is an excellent time to generate positive press for the school and the project. Students can prepare press releases and distribute them to newspapers as well as local radio and television stations. Be sure to check students' photo release eligibility and alert all photographers of any restrictions. A sample press release and photo release are found in Step 9.

- Divide the number of plants you have in your project design by the number of students.
- Students can plant an average of 10 quart sized plants an hour: less if the soil is hard, students are very young or the plants are larger. This includes the time it takes to dig the holes, and plant, water and mulch each plant. Even early elementary students are capable of planting multiple plants.
- Determine how many volunteers are necessary to assist students with the work. Younger students require the supervision of one adult for every five students, while older students may need one adult for every ten students. The greater the number of students participating at one time, the greater the number of overall volunteers you will need.
- Sometimes there is more interest among classes to participate than there is work to be done. In this case, plan an activity for some students to do while others have a chance to plant.
- Review all the tasks of planting day; be sure work is spread evenly throughout. Mulching and cleaning up will take time.

## Cityport Elementary School Work Plan

### One week before:

- Prepare and distribute a planting day schedule.
- Gather all needed materials.
- Contact the media.

### On planting day:

Mr. Moffett will greet each class, explain their tasks for the day, give a demonstration on how to properly plant and use tools safely, divide the class into small teams and distribute tools.

Mrs. Thompson will take photos of the planting throughout the day.

| Time | Teacher | Grade | Number of Students | Volunteers |
|------|---------|-------|--------------------|-----------|
| 7:30 – 8:30 | • Bring plants to project site. <br>• Stage plants and tools. <br>• Set up refreshment and first aid station. | | | Mr. Moffett (biologist) <br>Mrs. Soni (parent) <br>Mr. Sargent (parent II) |
| 8:45 – 9:30 | Mrs. Phillips | 2 | 20 | Mr. Moffett (biologist) <br>Mrs. Thompson (principal) <br>Mrs. Soni (parent) |
| 9:45 – 10:30 | Mr. Fiorey | 4 | 22 | Mr. Moffett (biologist) <br>Mrs. Thompson (principal) <br>Mrs. Soni (parent) |
| 10:45 – 11:30 | Ms. Strano | 5 | 23 | Mr. Moffett (biologist) <br>Mrs. Thompson (principal) <br>Mr. Sargent (parent II) <br>(Mrs. Soni lunch break) |
| 11:45 – 12:30 | Mrs. Li | 5 | 25 | Mr. Moffett (biologist) <br>Mrs. Silversmith (parent III) <br>Mrs. Soni (parent) <br>(Mrs. Thompson lunch break) |
| 12:45 – 1:30 | Ms. Bahner | 2 | 20 | Mrs. Silversmith (parent III) <br>Mrs. Thompson (principal) <br>Mrs. Soni (parent) <br>(Mr. Sargent lunch break) |
| 1:45 – 2:30 | Mr. Harper | 4 | 22 | Mr. Moffett (biologist) <br>Mrs. Thompson (principal) <br>Mrs. Soni (parent) |
| 2:45 – 3:30 | Mrs. Dieguez | 5 | 26 | Mr. Moffett (biologist) <br>Mrs. Thompson (principal) <br>Mrs. Soni (parent) |
| 3:30 – 4:30 | • Clean up tools and first aid station. <br>• Water plants. | | | Mr. Moffett (biologist) <br>Mrs. Soni (parent) <br>Mr. Sargent (parent II) |

*Cityport Elementary School's work plan includes important details for a successful work day.*

- Schedule breaks for your volunteers, especially if they are with you all day.

- Have students work in teams and take turns using the tools when working with larger sized plants.

- Students are always excited to try the tools that come with the job. Make sure you have enough tools for all of the students. Be sure to clearly mark any loaned equipment, so it can be returned when you are finished.

- Students are most excited about planting the plants, not mulching, watering or cleaning up. Make sure you have divided the plants so all students involved have the opportunity to put a plant in the ground.

- Keep safety first, have students and volunteers wear closed toed shoes, have adults use any motorized equipment and have a designated staffed area for questions, concerns, and first aid kits.

- Plan a back up volunteer day to finish up any leftover work.

# Gather Materials and Supplies

A formal order must be placed several weeks in advance to ensure that you have all the plants you need for planting day. Having a list of acceptable substitutions on hand will make finalizing the order go smoothly if the nursery does not have all the plants you anticipated being in stock. The day before your planting day, have your plants delivered. Make sure there are enough hands to do all the unloading. Keep the plants watered and in a safe, shady area where they will be stored until planting day. Have your plant list ready, and check

Frank Marsden

your order either when it is picked up or delivered. If you are unsure of what your plants will look like, ask the nursery to label them. On occasion, a nursery may substitute a different plant than what you ordered if it unexpectedly ran out of stock. Double check with the nursery that any substitute plants are native and suited for your site conditions.

# Plant Your Project

It's the moment we've all been waiting for. It's time to get dirty!

## Staging Plants

Staging is the term for laying out or spacing your plants throughout the project area prior to planting. This is done so that plants most closely match the project design. Both formal and informal project plans should be staged to ensure plants are put in their appropriate planting zones so they can thrive.

Plants can be staged in a number of different ways depending on the number and age of the students and the nature of your design. With older students, you may simply be able to use colored flags or marked stakes to delineate planting areas. If planting a wetland, raingarden or bioswale, plants should be grouped based on water tolerance. If planting a woodland or meadow, you may want to group plants based on the height they will attain when mature. For younger students, lay out individual plants. Allow older students to space out plants themselves.

Frank Marsden

### Tips for staging

Before staging plants, water them one more time if possible.

To avoid plant damage from students' feet during planting, stage plants for each group only after the previous group has left. If you will be planting an area backed by a wall or fence start planting along the barrier and work your way out. If you are planting an area that is open on all sides, start planting in the middle and work your way out.

## Donation Dangers

On occasion parents and volunteers will show up to planting days with plants from their homes as a gift to the school. Kindly place these plants aside until you can verify they would be appropriate choices for your project site. This website **http://www.aphis.usda.gov** provides a list of federally prohibited plants. You can cross reference the donation with this list and other local native plant guides.

## Planting Plants

Plants are purchased in containers, as seeds or as bare root seedlings. Appendix B has specific information on working with seeds. The most common technique for planting containerized plants and bare root trees will be described here.

### Plants and trees in containers

The smallest size is referred to as a plug and generally comes in trays of 50-75 plants from a wholesale nursery and a 4-6 pack from a retail nursery. Trays can be cut during the staging process, but plants should remain in their plastic sleeves until holes have been dug to prevent them from drying out. Larger plants that come in quart and gallon sized pots are typically one individual plant and should be planted whole.

When ready to plant, simply dig a hole deep enough so that the level of the existing soil is even with the level of soil the plant is in – not too deep, not too shallow. Remove the plant by gently squeezing the sides of the container and pushing up from the bottom. Then pull at the base of the stem until the plant comes loose. Place the plant in the hole and use the excess soil and any amendments to fill it back in. Gently pack or tamp the soil around the entire plant to fill in any existing air pockets. Assign a volunteer to check each plant to make sure this step has been completed correctly.

Some plants that are left in a container too long begin to grow their roots in a circular pattern around the inside edges of the container. This condition is known as root bound. Before planting a root bound plant, loosen the outside layer of roots until they are completely free of circling roots. For trees, the roots may be larger and require cutting with sheers or clippers.

### Bare root

Many trees are sold as bare root specimens and are planted with a dibble bar, as shown in the photo to the right. When planting bare root seedlings be sure they don't dry out while waiting by the planting hole. Take care to cover the roots with damp newspaper or straw or place them in a bucket of water.

*Container grown trees can be successfully planted for much of the year, while bare root trees must be planted during dormancy.*

USFWS

*If many of your purchased plants are root bound, put them aside and return them to the nursery for replacements. If plants have been root bound in containers for an extended period of time, their success in the ground is limited.*

Britt Eckhardt Slattery

## Tips for planting

- It is best for a trained volunteer to do a sample planting demonstration for each new group of students; this will help ensure plant survival. With younger students, it can be helpful to do one demonstration in the classroom and a second demonstration outside at the planting site. The most important part of planting is to make sure all participating students feel that they have contributed to their Schoolyard Habitat.

- Inexperienced students may need to be reminded to remove the plant from its pot. Provide any special instructions for items such as soil amendments and mulch. If you plan to mulch immediately following the planting, it can be helpful to place the plant containers upside down over the plants to protect them from getting buried or trampled. You can print and laminate the instruction card *Field Notes for Planting a Plant* supplied at the end of this step for team leaders and volunteers.

- During the planting day, step back and decide if things are taking the right shape. It is okay to make changes to your planting plan once you have begun as long as the plants stay within their planting zone requirements.

- Remove all stakes, strings and ribbons from the planting area except those depicting plant identification or being used as a temporary border from mowers.

- Water the plants as soon as they are planted. Then water them every day for at least one week unless there is rainfall.

*Commonly used by foresters, dibble bars can also be used by students to plant bare root seedlings.*

*The plant on the left is planted correctly. The plant on the right is too shallow.*

# Field Notes for Planting a Plant

## Procedure:

1. Dig a hole 2 to 3 times wider than the container and slightly deeper. Reserve removed soil next to the hole for use when backfilling.

2. Remove the plant from its container by lightly pressing against the sides of the container. If necessary, cut the container vertically to dislodge the root ball. Avoid breaking the root ball.

3. Lifting by the root ball, never by the stem or trunk, set the plant into the hole. Plants should be centered and level. Add compost or loosened soil back into the hole to allow the plant to be placed even with the original soil level.

4. Hold plant in place while backfilling around the root ball using reserved soil and compost. Press soil lightly to eliminate air pockets. Large dirt clods should be broken apart before backfilling.

5. Create a slightly indented watering saucer similar in size to the original hole. Add mulch as instructed. Do not mulch directly against the tree trunk or stem of the plant, doing so will cause the plant to rot.

6. Adequate water is essential at planting time. If told to do so, water at the base of the plant until the soil is saturated.

7. Clean and return all tools to the staging area.

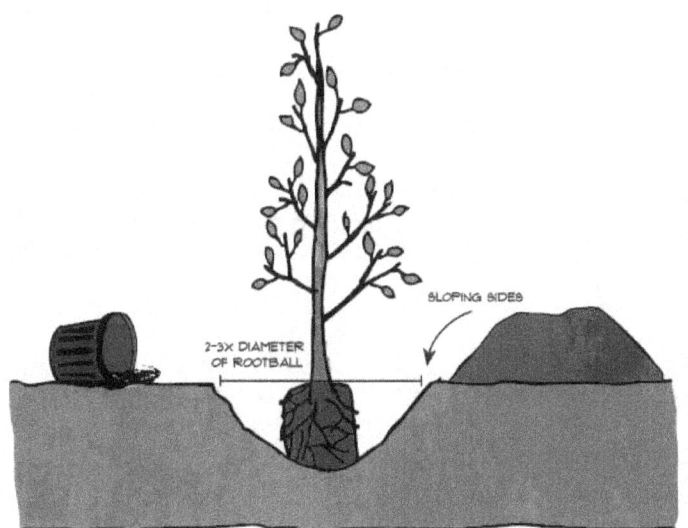

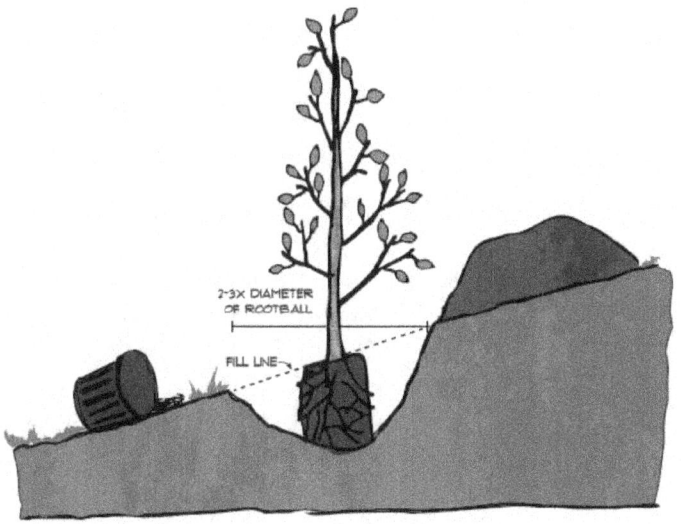

**Tip:** Do not remove tree from container until you are ready to place into planting hole. Fine roots dry out rapidly when exposed to air and can cause the plant to die.

*"Keep a green tree in your heart and perhaps a songbird will come."*

— *Chinese proverb*

# INCORPORATE

## Steps 7 – 9

A Schoolyard Habitat project is much more than the planting day. Your project is the representation of the relationship between your school community and its environment.

This is the shortest section of the guide but the longest commitment for your team. The completion of these steps is unique and personal to your school and your project. Maintaining, using and sharing are the universal steps that help sustain every project because they provide opportunities each year for new students to become stewards of the schoolyard. How these steps are developed will depend entirely on the specific elements that make your project and school community unique.

The incorporation of the project ensures that all your hard work will pay off. This is critically important because it is the legacy of your project. You used the schoolyard as a teaching tool throughout the assessment of your school grounds and implementation of your project. Now is the time to fully integrate the project into the culture of the school, so that generations of students will continue to immerse themselves in the living resources of the Schoolyard Habitat. The viability of this project as a teaching tool and wildlife habitat will continue if you take the steps to incorporate the project into the school community now.

*"To forget how to dig the earth and tend the soil is to forget ourselves."*

*— Mahatma Gandhi*

# STEP SEVEN:
# Create a Maintenance Plan

Schoolyard Habitat projects are generally lower maintenance landscapes if ecologically sound. Most maintenance involves controlling unwanted plants, maintaining structures, removing trash and preserving aesthetics. Choose how much you want to maintain based on the availability of your team members' time and the maintenance requirements of the different features. For example, if you have a two acre woodland restoration with a trail, you might have a more intensive maintenance plan for the entrance to the trail than you do for the majority of the forest.

There are essentially two levels of care that every project needs. Short-term maintenance includes watering, mulching, borders, weeding and replanting. Long-term maintenance includes invasive non-native species removal, care of structures and other project features. All maintenance provides an opportunity to engage students in learning more about their natural environment.

## Accomplishments

☑ Committed to Starting a Project
☑ Formed a Team
☑ Developed a Master Plan
☑ Assessed Project Site
☑ Designed Project
☑ Decided Money Matters
☑ Installed Project

## Tasks

☐ Consider short-term maintenance
☐ Consider long-term maintenance

7

# Consider Short-term Maintenance

The first two years after installation are the most critical and labor intensive time for maintenance. A maintenance plan for the first two years should include specific tasks and indicate who will be responsible for them. This is a good time to recruit new members to your team. Below are aspects to consider when creating your plan.

## Watering

Watering is the most important short-term maintenance task. Plan to monitor the rainfall and augment with watering or irrigation when needed for at least the first two years of your project. This is especially important during hot, dry summer months when staff and students are not at school. Water sufficiently and deeply but not too often. Thorough watering promotes stronger root systems, enabling plants to find water on their own once established.

Your watering plan could involve as much as installing drip irrigation or a sprinkler system, or as little as laying a soaker hose or using a hose with a sprinkler attachment. Establish a watering schedule with advice from the nursery from which you acquired the plants. On average, a newly planted habitat needs one inch of water per week for the first one to two years.

Your school's maintenance staff should be part of the team to ensure there is access to water especially for the summer. Many schools require a special water key to operate outdoor spigots; these can be found in the plumbing section of your local hardware store. You may want to install a simple rain gauge at your project site to help monitor watering needs. Trees and shrubs need to be watered through the first two years. Many home and garden stores sell irrigation bags, often called tree gators, specifically for trees and shrubs. They can be filled with a hose once a week and provide a slow drip irrigation to the plant.

## Mulching

Once plants are established the need for mulch becomes obsolete. In many naturalized areas the annual deadfall will act as natural mulch. If you choose to add mulch for aesthetic reasons, refer to the calculations in Step 4 to find out how much you will need. Keep in mind that too thick a layer of mulch will prevent moisture from reaching the ground.

## Borders

One of the most common frustrations for a Schoolyard Habitat project occurs when it is accidently mowed. It is helpful to mark off the area of your project to let the maintenance team and visitors know the boundaries. To indicate the boundaries of your project, you can use fencing, edging or natural materials. Find out if the maintenance personnel changes in the summer so that all staff are aware of the project.

## Weeding

To improve the wildlife habitat of your school grounds, it is imperative that you eliminate invasive non-native plants. Weeding your project can sometimes seem daunting, especially when native species are young and hard to recognize. Keep in mind that not every species that springs up into your project is unwanted. Some plants that are native to the area could colonize the project site. As long as the colonizing plants are not invasive, it is fine to leave them alone.

*Summer weeding and watering are common challenges of Schoolyard Habitat projects. Be sure you have a plan in place to address this challenge.*

The problem occurs when invasive non-native species are found in your habitat. These species will take over and must be removed as quickly as possible. This website **http://www.aphis.usda.gov** provides a list of federally prohibited plants. You can cross reference any new plants you find with this list and other local native plant guides. It can also be helpful to have your planting map accessible during weeding.

## Replanting

The survival rate of your plants will need to be evaluated in the first few months. Some plant loss can be expected. Replanting makes sense if the plant loss was caused by something unlikely to occur again such as an extreme weather event. If plant loss is more than 50%, evaluate the reason for the loss before replanting to maximize future success. The natural resource professional on your team can evaluate your site and offer suggestions for successful future plantings.

> For more information about invasive species refer to the
> Invasive Plant Atlas of the United States **http://www.invasiveplantatlas.org**
> or the National Park Service **www.nps.gov/plants/alien/factmain.htm**

# Consider Long-term Maintenance

For as long as the property remains a Schoolyard Habitat, some level of maintenance must be done.

## Invasive Non-Native Species Removal

The best method for keeping invasive plants out of your project area is early detection and immediate removal. Common control methods include hand pulling, mowing, chemical spraying or solarizing. Your invasive non-native species maintenance plan will depend on the specific invasive plant, the size of the patch and the amount of surrounding native vegetation. Contact your local master gardeners' group or county extension office to find a weed control specialist to help with assessment and treatment options.

## Maintenance tips for invasive non-natives:

Frank Marsden

- Create a "Most Unwanted" species lists with identification features of the plants to help know which plants to remove.

- For most weeds, hand pulling is enough. Be sure to remove the entire plant both above and below the ground prior to the plant going to seed.

- Chemical methods for removing invasive non-native plants include a broadcast spray which will kill all plants in a large area or spot treatment which is applied to a specific problem plant only. Most school systems have protocols and licensed personnel for herbicide applications.

- If your project site has become overgrown with unwanted plants, you may want to tag species worth saving and have volunteers weed around the base of these plants to allow room for growth.

## Structures and other features

Check feeders, birdbaths, water pumps, artificial structures, benches and signs to make sure mechanisms are functioning properly and vandalism has not compromised the integrity of the feature. With vandalism, trash and other issues, constant vigilance keeps an area looking good. The best way to decrease the likelihood that the site will be vandalized is to increase the support and participation of the students and community. Creating a sense of shared ownership and responsibility will provide multiple benefits for the project.

## Sample Maintenance Plans

Exact timing and specific tasks will be determined by your project type and location. Below you will find some sample maintenance plans to help figure out your annual maintenance needs and help delineate the roles of each member of the Schoolyard Habitat team once the project is in the ground.

*In this sample, the responsible party is ensuring that the task will be completed, the assisting party will help complete the task and the consulting party would be part of any decision making regarding that task.*

| FIRST TWO YEARS | | | | |
|---|---|---|---|---|
| Category | Tasks | Responsible | Assist | Consult |
| Water | Monitor weekly rainfall | Mrs. Jones's 6th grade class and Mrs. Hogan's Summer Habitat Scouts | PTA members | Maintenance supervisor and Assistant Principal |
| | Monthly check on irrigation equipment including timers and hoses | Maintenance supervisor | Assistant Principal | Schoolyard Habitat Team |
| Plants | Monthly monitoring and removal of invasive non-natives | Mrs. Jones's 6th grade class and Mrs. Hogan's Summer Habitat Scouts | Schoolyard Habitat Team | Maintenance supervisor and Assistant Principal |
| | Every spring new trees are planted to replace any mortality from previous year | Mr. Casey's 8th grade class | Schoolyard Habitat Team | Maintenance supervisor and Assistant Principal |
| Structure | Monthly monitoring and reporting of any vandalism issues | Schoolyard Habitat Team | PTA members | Assistant Principal |
| ONGOING | | | | |
| Category | Tasks | Responsible | Assist | Consult |
| Plants | Monthly monitoring and removal of invasive non-natives | Mrs. Jones's 6th grade class and Mrs. Hogan's Summer Habitat Scouts | Schoolyard Habitat Team | Maintenance supervisor and Assistant Principal |
| Structure | Benches, sign and fence are repaired as needed | Maintenance supervisor | Assistant Principal | Schoolyard Habitat Team |
| | Trail head is mulched and trail maps are in stock | Mrs. Hogan's Summer Habitat Scouts | Schoolyard Habitat Team | Assistant Principal |

*In this sample, maintenance needs are laid out by time of year. Short-term needs should be completed for the first two years, and long-term needs extend through the life of the project.*

| SHORT-TERM | MONTH | LONG-TERM |
|---|---|---|
| Water as necessary. | January | Clean out nest boxes. |
| Water as necessary. | February | |
| Weed, remove invasive species. Water as necessary. | March | Monitor and remove invasive species. |
| Monitor species survival rates. Water as necessary. | April | |
| Weed and add mulch if needed. Water as necessary. | May | |
| Water as necessary. | June | |
| Water as necessary. | July | Monitor for drought. |
| Water as necessary. | August | |
| Weed and remove invasive species. Water as necessary. | September | Monitor and remove invasive species. |
| Monitor species survival rates and prepare for additional planting if necessary. Water as necessary. | October | |
| Water as necessary. | November | Mow half of meadow. |
| Water as necessary. | December | |

# STEP EIGHT:
## Use the Project

Now that the project is installed and being maintained, there are likely to be even more opportunities for using the project than you had first imagined. Revisit your goals and consider all of the ways you can use the project in your school's curriculum. Consider other groups within your school community who may be interested in using the project. Revisit your master plan and think about what project should be next.

**Accomplishments**
- ☑ Committed to Starting a Project
- ☑ Formed a Team
- ☑ Developed a Master Plan
- ☑ Assessed Project Site
- ☑ Designed Project
- ☑ Decided Money Matters
- ☑ Installed Project
- ☑ Created a Maintenance Plan

**Tasks**
- ☐ Brainstorm Ways for Using the Schoolyard Habitat
- ☐ Provide Teacher Professional Development
- ☐ Monitor for Change

# Brainstorm Ways for Using the Schoolyard Habitat

Look at entire outcomes of the grade level or subject matter, not just the environmental ones. Identify outcomes that can be brought alive in an outdoor setting. For example read a book in your habitat whose story takes place outside such as *The Hungry Caterpillar* or *Lord of the Flies*. Identify abstract concepts that could be enhanced with a concrete context such as measuring angles, estimating distance, sorting and listing, creating a still-life, writing a persuasive essay and identifying changes over time.

Network with other schools that have created and use their Schoolyard Habitats. Find out how and when they are able to integrate the habitat into their curriculum.

The Schoolyard Habitat project can be integrated into extracurricular or afterschool activities; the trails can be a part of the cross country trail, or an art or photography club could use the project as a setting. As the users of the project grow, then the project itself becomes more integrated into the school community.

# Provide Teacher Professional Development

Training the school staff on the use of the schoolyard will help ensure that the money and time your school has invested in the project will be put to good use. Talk to your school administrators about sponsoring regular teacher trainings on how to use the project to meet curricular standards. Consider the following options:

• Use a half day training session to review activities for each grade level that can be used in conjunction with the project.

• Contact your local environmental education center to arrange for a demonstration of how teachers can use the habitat with their students.

USFWS

USFWS

USFWS

# Monitor for Change

Develop a monitoring plan to assess the change of wildlife use and habitat. Monitoring plans should include ways to track and record changes over time. Monitoring plans will evolve as the years progress. Older students can create and investigate their own interests based on previous years' data and with help, even very young students can investigate the habitat.

USFWS

### Some of the monitoring possibilities

- Seasons
- Weather
- Phenology
- Temperature
- Migration
- Phases of the moon
- Abundance and diversity of plants, insects, birds and mammals
- Different life stages of plants and animals
- Succession
- Signs of wildlife (nests, tracks, or scat)
- Surface and ground water quality

To explore some of the possibilities for your next project look at what the monitoring data is telling you are the needs of the ecological community. Revisit your goals and master plan and consider what may need to be changed or what phase should be implemented next.

Cindy Landers

## Collect and Share

Share your data using online networks such as the National Phenology Network, GLOBE, Migration Watch, Earth Partnership for Schools and others.

*"A nation that destroys its soils destroys itself. Forests are the lungs of our land, purifying the air and giving fresh strength to our people."*

*— Franklin Delano Roosevelt*

SCHOOLYARD HABITAT PROJECT GUIDE

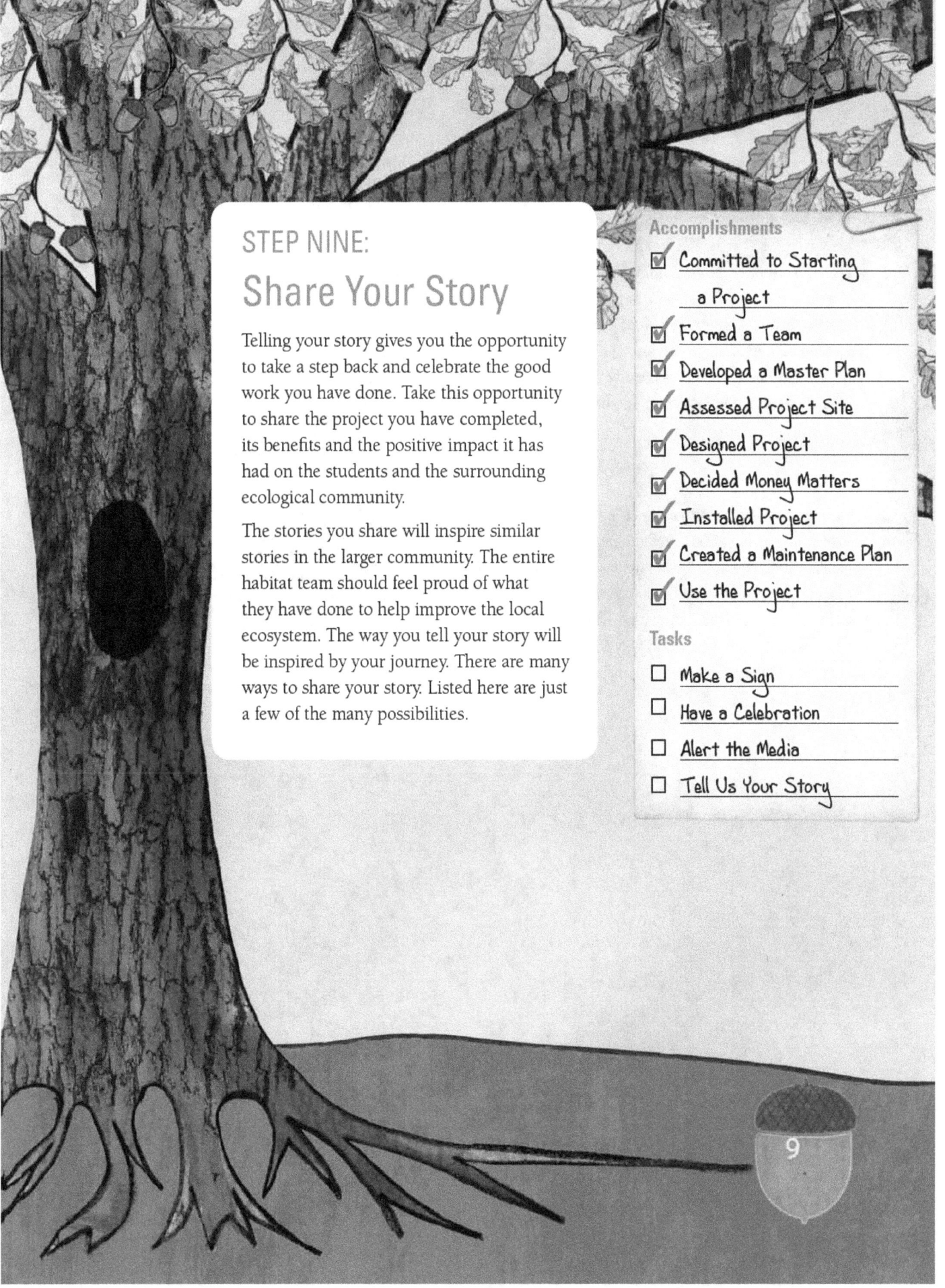

## STEP NINE:
# Share Your Story

Telling your story gives you the opportunity to take a step back and celebrate the good work you have done. Take this opportunity to share the project you have completed, its benefits and the positive impact it has had on the students and the surrounding ecological community.

The stories you share will inspire similar stories in the larger community. The entire habitat team should feel proud of what they have done to help improve the local ecosystem. The way you tell your story will be inspired by your journey. There are many ways to share your story. Listed here are just a few of the many possibilities.

### Accomplishments

- ☑ Committed to Starting a Project
- ☑ Formed a Team
- ☑ Developed a Master Plan
- ☑ Assessed Project Site
- ☑ Designed Project
- ☑ Decided Money Matters
- ☑ Installed Project
- ☑ Created a Maintenance Plan
- ☑ Use the Project

### Tasks

- ☐ Make a Sign
- ☐ Have a Celebration
- ☐ Alert the Media
- ☐ Tell Us Your Story

9

## Make a Sign

Signs should reach out to your entire community and be easy to read, sturdy and weatherproof. Consider using the sign to share general information on the benefits of the project as well as specific information such as species names. It may be required to post rules for access and appropriate use. Signs can be student or professionally made. The cost of a professionally made sign is high but often lasts much longer than handmade ones.

## Have a Celebration

Celebrating is a great way to recognize the effort everyone has contributed to the project. Ideas for celebrations include ribbon cutting ceremonies, tours of the habitat and appreciation certificates. Remember to include all project supporters. Linking celebrations with clean up days is a great way to encourage continued support for your project.

*Signs are an excellent opportunity to recognize the partners who supported the project.*

*Allow students to celebrate their journey by sending habitat stories and thank you letters.*

# Alert the Media

## Writing a Press Release

A press release is a way for you to inform television and radio stations, websites and newspapers about your project. A press release should contain enough information so that it can be used without the newsperson calling back for more facts. Before writing the press release, decide the purpose of the release and the most interesting aspects of the story. The first paragraph should answer the basic questions - who, what, where, when and why (and sometimes how). Additional paragraphs can provide more detailed information. When writing a press release, keep the following in mind:

• The press release should capture the attention of a reporter or editor;

• Tell the most important part of the story in the lead (first paragraph);

• After the lead, elaborate on details;

• Keep press releases short (40 or fewer sentences);

• Follow the basic style below.

Release time: Flush left and underlined, type "For release on" and add the date you want the news media to publish the release or type "For immediate release" if you want it published as soon as the news media receive it.

Contact: Flush right, type name and phone number of a person the press can contact for more information. Make sure the contact person will be available and responsive to calls.

Title: Centered, bold face type identifies content of the release; use an action verb like "plant."

Body: Double spaced. First sentence of each paragraph should be indented. Do not break sentences or paragraphs between pages. For releases longer than one page, the word "more" should be centered at bottom of first page. End releases with 3 Xs (with spaces between) or the word "END" centered at the bottom.

## Sample Media Release

 Cityport Elementary School • 783 Cool School Lane • Birdstown, CA 99999

FOR IMMEDIATE RELEASE:
December 22, 2010

For Information Contact:
Dawson McCabe (123) 333-1234

Students Going Wild At School

Fifth graders at Cityport Elementary School in Birdstown, CA, are doing more than reading about wildlife; they are creating homes for wildlife right on the schoolyard. On April 20, from 9 a.m. to noon, students, teachers and local citizens will plant more than 50 trees and shrubs in their schoolyard to create a woodland to allow wildlife to thrive in an area once covered by asphalt.

Once established, the woodland will provide food, water, cover and nesting area to a variety of birds, amphibians, small mammals and other wildlife. Besides providing homes for wildlife, the woodland can be used by students and teachers as an outdoor classroom. Students will have the opportunity to learn about wildlife and the environment and to conduct scientific experiments without even leaving the school grounds.

"These students are really excited about actually creating habitat for wildlife," said Logan Kelly, the fifth grade teacher. "We're thankful for the support of the entire community."

Directions: From Sacramento take Route 50 east to Exit 42. At first stoplight, turn right onto Cool School Lane. Follow to school.

x x x

# Tell Us Your Story

## Tell Us Your Story and Receive a Schoolyard Habitat Project Sign

The U.S. Fish and Wildlife Service is providing signs to schools to identify Schoolyard Habitat projects throughout the nation. The information you submit will be entered into a database and used to promote Schoolyard Habitat efforts. Any woodland, meadow or wetland project qualifies for a sign.

Please fill out the following questions with brief responses and return to: Schoolyard Habitat Program, U.S. Fish and Wildlife Service, 2800 Cottage Way Suite 1916, Sacramento, CA 95825 or R8SchoolYardHabitat@fws.gov

**schoolyard habitat program**

**Students Restoring Wildlife Habitat**

Project support from the U.S. Fish & Wildlife Service
www.fws.gov/cno/conservation/schoolyard.cfm

### Tell us where you are and what you did:

1. School Name & Website if applicable _____

    Address: _____

    Phone #: _____

    Contact: _____

2. Date Project Started _____ Date Completed _____

3. What grade level students were involved? How many? _____

4. Describe the type of project(s) you completed and the size of each project in square feet.

    _____

    _____

    _____

    _____

5. List any other habitat features added to the project including the following: nesting boxes, brush piles, trails, outdoor seating area etc. _____

    _____

    _____

    _____

    _____

*continued on other side...*

**Tell us a little more about your schoolyard work:**

6.  What is most successful about your project?_____
_____
_____
_____

7.  What is the most challenging aspect of your project? _____
_____
_____
_____

8.  How were students involved in planning and installing the project? _____
_____
_____
_____

9.  Do you have plans for future projects? If so, describe. _____
_____
_____
_____

10. How do you use the habitat for instruction? _____
_____
_____
_____

11. How did you receive this guide? _____
_____
_____
_____

12. What part of this guide was the most use to you?_____
_____
_____
_____

13. Please include any photos with proper photo releases you would like us to consider using.

# Agreement for Use of Likeness in Service Products

## ☐ *Grant Unrestricted Use of Likeness*

I hereby grant permission to the U.S. Fish and Wildlife Service (USFWS) to make visual and/or audio recordings of myself and/or any minor under my control at the time of the recording. I also grant permission to the USFWS to use these photographic, video and/or audio recordings in official Service publications, productions, displays and on the Internet without any consideration. I hereby irrevocably authorize the USFWS to edit, alter, copy, exhibit, publish or distribute this photo/video/audio for any lawful purpose. I understand these photo/video/audio recordings will be in the public domain.

As a result of being in the public domain, theUSFWS, or anyone else, may freely publish, reproduce, use and/or distribute these photo/video/audio recordings in any media without your approval or permission, with no monetary compensation to you and without temporal or geographic restriction (unless using your likeness for commercial use - then your permission is required).

In addition, I waive the right to inspect or approve the finished product, including written or electronic copy, where in my likeness appears. I also hereby hold harmless and release and forever discharge the USFWS from all claims, demands, and causes of action which I, my heirs, representatives, executors, administrators, or any other persons, acting on my behalf or on behalf of my estate have or may have by reason of this authorization, and agree to indemnify the USFWS, its officers, agents and employees against any out of pocket expenses, including attorney's fees, that may be incurred in defense against any such claim, action or proceeding. I am at least 18 years of age and am competent to contract in my own name. I have read this release before signing below and fully understand the content, meaning, and impact of this release.

## ☐ *Grant Restricted Use of Likeness*

I hereby allow the USFWS to use my likeness, and/or the likeness of any minor under my control at the time of the recording, in Service publications, productions, displays, the Internet, etc, with the following conditions:

---

Print Name of Minor

| Print Name | Signature | Date | Phone or E-mail |

*Service Representative*_____ *Office*_____ *Phone*_____

FWS Form 3-2260  01/2011

*"The unutterable beauty of a blossom. The grace of a high-flying bird. The roar of wind in the trees; At one time or another in our lives nature touches you...and me...and all of us in some personal, special way."*

*— Joseph Cornell*

# CONGRATULATIONS

Consider the effects of the habitat project on your students and school community. Collect and catalogue information using surveys, test scores and attendance, as well as student's own reflections to assess these impacts.

With your team, review the project master plan and goals and decide what project will be next!

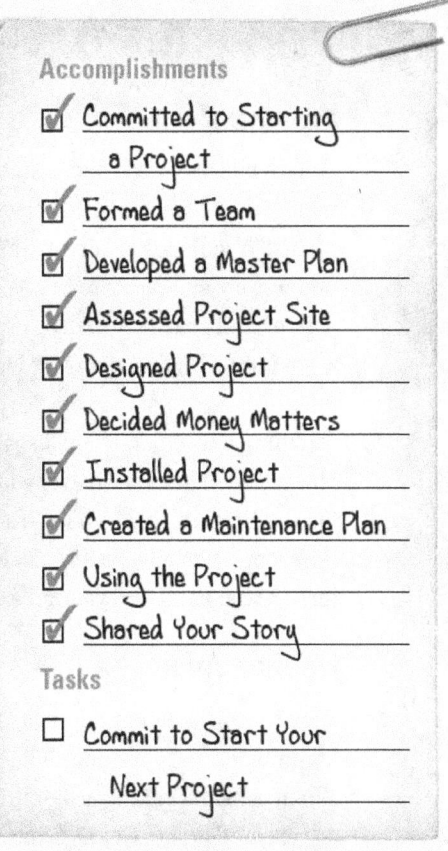

**Accomplishments**

☑ Committed to Starting a Project

☑ Formed a Team

☑ Developed a Master Plan

☑ Assessed Project Site

☑ Designed Project

☑ Decided Money Matters

☑ Installed Project

☑ Created a Maintenance Plan

☑ Using the Project

☑ Shared Your Story

**Tasks**

☐ Commit to Start Your Next Project

# Appendix A: Woodland

## Woodland

Woodlands are areas dominated by large trees but also include many other plants such as shrubs, small trees and herbaceous plants. Woodlands or forests, have a canopy, mid-layer, understory and floor. Each layer provides a wide range of food, shelter and space for many animals. A mature woodland floor is covered with decomposing leaves and trees. Logs and brush piles are also a part of a healthy woodland habitat. When you walk into a woodland, you'll see that the layers blend together. Not all woodlands have every layer. Climate, soil and other factors determine which layers develop in a woodland. All of the different parts of a woodland are important. Together they will form a woodland ecosystem.

Frank Marsden

## Habitat Value

A mature woodlands' many layers provide unique habitat for a wide variety of insects, birds, amphibians and mammals. Certain plants provide specific habitat niches for many of these critters. When considering the ecological impact of a plant species in your woodland, remember not all plants are created equal. Contact your local forester for more information on your area. For most of the woodlands in the United States, locally native oaks, willows and pines provide high value habitat for native wildlife.

## Step 4: Design Considerations

When selecting plants for your woodland, be sure to include evergreens, shrubs and groundcover. In a natural woodland, you will notice trees are not spaced evenly or found in straight lines. Your restoration site should follow this rule as well. Resist the temptation to space trees in rows. However, if your school requires the understory to be mowed, be sure to space the trees wider than the width of the school's mower.

Weed matting can be installed to protect the base of the trees from weed encroachment. Sometimes tree stakes can be used to support young trees, and protective tubes can provide support and deter damage from browsing wildlife such as deer and rodents. These additions should only be considered if recommended by the natural resource professional on your team.

Follow the directions in "Calculating number of plants needed" to determine how many trees and shrubs you need. The NRCS recommends planting about 374 trees per acre.

## Step 7: Maintenance Considerations

### Watering

There are two techniques specific to watering woodland plantings: drip irrigation and water gel packs. Use these methods to apply the recommended watering rates for newly established plantings. Consult your natural resource professional to determine what type of watering regime, if any, is needed.

### Mulching

Mulch is not necessary for a woodland planting; however, if you want to delineate seedling locations, spread 2 to 3 inches of leaves or woodchips around each seedling.

### Mowing and Pruning

Woodlands do not require mowing or pruning. For appearance, some schools choose to mow between trees until they are established.

### Weeding

Other plants will colonize the site. This is a natural process that will add to the diversity of your woodland. If the colonizing plants are not invasive, it is best to leave them alone.

### Invasive Species Removal

For woodland plantings, invasive vines can become problematic. Monitor the woodland and remove any invasive vine that starts growing up the seedlings. Once trees are established, they will shade out many undesirable species decreasing the need to remove them.

*High school students are empowered through participation in large scale restoration projects.*

# Appendix B: Meadow

## Meadow

Meadows are comprised of flowers, grasses, roots and decaying vegetation from previous years' growth. In the central United States, they are referred to as prairies. In much of the rest of the United States, meadows are transitional and if left alone would eventually evolve into a scrub-shrub habitat and then a woodland. Meadows are known for their striking colors and textures. Meadows provide dense cover for ground-nesting birds and burrowing animals and provide space for many insects including important pollinators. The rule of thumb for restoring meadows is sleep, creep and leap. During the first year after planting a meadow, weeds often dominate the site with the meadow plants hiding underneath (sleep). Seeds germinate but put most of their growth into their root systems. In fact, 60% to 90% of a plant's biomass is formed underground during the first year (creep). It isn't until year three or four when you'll notice the plants thriving above ground (leap).

Frank Marsden

## Habitat Value

The grasses of a meadow provide structural support with their dense, thick stems and fibrous root systems that can extend beyond 10 feet underground. Flowers provide important food sources with their blooms, leaves and seeds. Grazing insects such as grasshoppers, leafhoppers and butterfly larvae feed on meadow grasses and flowers. Some plant species provide for a larger variety of insects than others. Check with local experts such as your county extension office or university entomologist to find out more about what native species are most important in your area. Birds feed on these insects as well as highly nutritious seeds produced by meadow plants. Meadow plants provide cover and places to nest, as well as wind protection for many smaller species.

## Step 4: Design Considerations

Selecting a variety of flowers and grasses will provide visual interest, food for wildlife and enhanced diversity. When determining a ratio of grasses to flowers, consider cost, ecology and aesthetics of the site. Natural resource professionals tend to design meadow mixes with 30% to 60% grasses. A low proportion of grasses (30% or less of total plants) increases the intensity of the floral display, though this will often increase the cost.

> ### Meadows are Much More Than a "No-Mow Zone"
> A "no mow zone" or an area that is simply unmaintained allows any exisiting vegetation to grow tall.
> A meadow is the purposeful establishment of native plants that have a high habitat value.

One of the most dramatic phenological sequences in a meadow is the blooming of plants from mid-April through October. In historic native prairies, a new flower comes into bloom about every week during the growing season. To mimic this sequence, you must plant 30 or more different flower species. However, if your space is limited, you could plant a minimum of 15 flowers and 3 grasses and still have an ecologically functioning meadow.

### Finding Seeds

Use perennial species and purchase seeds from a reputable source that allows you to choose specific species or has a choice of locally native seed mixes. Do not use prepared seed mixes sold at lawn and garden stores as they tend to have a high percentage of annual, and sometimes invasive non-native species. Also, avoid purchasing seed mixes or "seed mats" that don't list the flower species on their package.

You can choose to collect seeds from the wild, but make sure you obtain permission from the landowner first. Never collect more than 25% of the seed available in any one wild spot. This will leave enough seeds to germinate in the next year. Collecting plant seeds from an area that is planned for development would be the exception to the 25% collection rule.

### Seeding Rates

The seeding rate is the amount of seed applied to a given area, usually shown as lbs/acre or oz/sq ft. The seeding rate is based on the pure live seed (PLS) content of your mixture. Seed purchased from a reputable dealer will have the PLS content on the packaging, as well as the recommended seeding rate. For wild collected seed, use the rates recommended by seed dealers and then err to the excessive. It will not hurt your project to have too much seed.

## Step 6: Meadow Installation

### Site Preparation

Existing weeds and sod are the biggest barriers to successful meadow establishment. It is recommended to use herbicide to prepare your site as it is the most effective way to eliminate exisiting vegetation without disturbing the soil or weed seeds. If herbicide is not possible, determine which of the sod removal techniques from Step 6 you will use.

## Plant Economics

For small sites, establishing your meadow with plants rather than seed will give you quicker results. However, this costs more and fewer species are available in containers. An alternative would be to have students raise the plants from seeds and transplant them to the habitat.

### Seeding Technique

**1. Prepare the seeds.**

Many of the seeds you will be working with are very small. Several thousand seeds per ounce is not uncommon. To evenly distribute such tiny seeds, it is necessary to dilute them by mixing them with a suitable material, such as dampened sand or sawdust. Use a volume of sand or sawdust equal to or greater than the volume of your seeds. The more you dilute your seed mixture, the more students you can involve in the planting activity.

**2. Distribute the seeds.**

Divide the mixture in half. Distribute half of the mixture to the students and have them broadcast the seeds gradually while walking across the site. Use the second half of the mixture and broadcast the seeds while walking perpendicular to the first path. This process will allow for an even distribution of the seed mixture.

**3. Tamp the seeds.**

Good soil contact is important for germination success. Have the students walk, stomp or dance back and forth across the site, or rent a lawn roller to gently push the seed mixture into the soil surface. Burying the seed is not your goal. Many of these seeds require light to germinate.

**4. Protect the seeds.**

Seed germination is increased if straw is lightly spread across the site and kept moist.

### Seed Dispersal

For sites of an acre or more, consider using a tractor with a seed drill and also have students broadcast seeds as described above. Contact your local NRCS office for availability. An operator will come with the tractor and will know how to calibrate the machine. This will ensure the entire site is planted and the students are involved.

## Step 7: Maintenance Considerations

The first two years of establishing a meadow is the most intensive time for maintenance. During this time, you are tying to eliminate the growth of woody species and annual weeds.

*Controlled burning is an achievable option for meadow maintenance.*

## Watering

Meadows only need to be watered during the first two years of establishment, if at all. They are most commonly watered using a sprinkler system. Make sure that the water soaks deeply into the ground. Intermittent deep watering is more beneficial to the plants than many short, shallow waterings.

## Mowing and Pruning

Mowing eliminates annual weeds before they go to seed and will not harm new wildflower seedlings and native grasses. If weeds are not evident, mowing is not necessary. Where a lot of weeds are growing, mow to a height of 6 to 8 inches every six weeks during the growing season. This will encourage the growth of the native perennials and discourage the growth of annuals that were not seeded. After mowing, remove cut material and thatch. This practice opens the soil to light, promoting the growth of new meadow plants. On small sites, removing thatch can be done by hand using a rake or on large sites by using a mechanical rake pulled behind a tractor.

Beyond the first year, annual mowing on a rotating schedule is needed if weeds are present. Be sure to schedule mowing prior to nesting season. Mowing should be done in small sections at a time, or in a mosaic of strips with unmowed sections in between. Mowing one-third of the site each year assures that some year round cover remains available for wildlife.

Pruning dead flower heads is optional. It may improve appearance, but it removes seeds that would germinate or provide food and cover in your habitat.

## Burning

Controlled burns are used to mimic the natural patterns that meadows have evolved to withstand. This technique has been used on school grounds to remove thatch and control woody species and promote new growth. Burning should be done on a rotation similar to the recommended mowing schedule. Strict precautions are necessary, contact your local fire department or natural resource agency; they will help you through preparation, required permitting and oversight of a controlled burn.

# Appendix C: Wetland

## Wetland

All wetlands have three characteristics: water, saturated soil and plants adapted to wet conditions. Depending on the region of the United States, different types of wetlands are found including marshes, swamps, prairie potholes and vernal pools. A marsh is the wettest type of wetland and is dominated by herbaceous plants such as cattails. A swamp is a wetland dominated by trees. Wetlands provide important habitat to many species as well as important water quality benefits. Because of the complex nature of wetlands, a natural resource professional will be required to help design, acquire permits and install your project.

*Planting a wetland is fun and sometimes very messy. Be sure your students and volunteers are prepared with extra clothes and a relaxed attitude.*

## Habitat Value

Wetlands prevent floods by slowing down rainwater running off the land. They also filter pollutants including toxins, excess nutrients and sediment. Wetlands have varying levels of water, types of vegetation and decomposing plant material that provide essential habitat to many different wildlife species to hide, nest, eat and bask. Creating a wetland provides one of the most immediate habitat transformations. Dragonflies, frogs and birds will move into the habitat shortly after creation.

## Step 4: Design Considerations

### Water Tolerance

A wetland will have varying water depth zones including upland, transition and standing water. Each depth zone will require specific plants with the proper water tolerance. It is important to know the water tolerance of each species and the anticipated water levels within the project site. Too little or too much water and improperly placed species will greatly affect the survival rate. Your local native wetland plant nursery will be able to help you choose species for specific water depths.

### Shape and Topography

If existing soils are suitable for a natural wetland, your shape can be as freeform as you would like. Curves, dips, points, coves and islands provide more shoreline and better hiding places for animals. Keep in mind the necessary excavation methods, the cost of excavation and the amount of detail that will be feasible with large equipment. You may want to ask an excavation contractor to create contours, dips and islands in the middle of the wetland. If your soils are not suitable for a natural wetland and a lining material is necessary, then you may be limited to circular or rectangular shapes.

## Size and Depth

Wetland size and depth is determined by your goals, space, hydrology and budget. Most wetlands created on schoolyards are 1 to 3 feet in depth. Check with your local natural resource professional to determine the size and depth your wetland should be to match your goals and site conditions. Consider creating a seasonal wetland if you live in an area where rainfall or snow melt is not adequate to keep water in your wetland year round. Some counties or school districts may have concerns or regulations about the depth of your wetland. Keep in mind public and private schools from across the country have been able to construct wetlands on their schoolyard.

## Profile

Wetlands with gradual slopes allow for the establishment of a diverse plant community and easy access for wildlife and students. A ratio of 4 feet horizontal run for every 1 foot of vertical depth is sufficient. Some sides of your wetland may be steeper and some flatter if needed. Shelves can be created in wetlands with deeper areas to help with safety concerns.

## Stormwater Management

Wetlands are one way to address storm-water management on your schoolyard. You may also consider creating improvements through green infrastructure. Though they can be considered a schoolyard habitat project, these types of projects may be much more complex in design. These programs are often intended to improve water quality through more extensive management of storm-water runoff. Some examples of green infrastructure include:

- permeable pavements in parks, basketball courts and parking lots
- raingardens and bioretention systems
- constructed wetlands for storm-water management or wastewater treatment
- green roofs and vertical or living walls

## Wetland Liners

If you discover your soil will not hold water, you must then modify the excavation with a lining material. This method should only be used if recommended by a natural resource professional and the benefits of curricular outcomes and habitat value outweigh the cost of project. When designing a wetland with a liner, remember to over-excavate to allow for returning at least 8 inches of top soil back into the hole. This will provide a good substrate for the roots of the wetland plants. There are three main types of liners to choose from: clay, synthetic and preform. Liners can be quite heavy and require special techniques to handle and install.

**Clay Liners:** Clay is the best material for installing a liner, is typically used to increase the amount of water an area can hold, and can be used on any size site. Natural clay is applied in a uniform layer 6 to 12 inches thick throughout the wetland area, then compacted to form a sealed layer. You will need to excavate a minimum of 16 inches to allow space for the layers of clay and top soil needed to bring your wetland back to its designed depth and contour. For a 2 foot wetland, excavate at least 40 inches deep and use the excess soil as a planting layer inside the liner. Remember to maintain a gradual 4:1 slope along the wetland edge.

Bentonite, a processed clay product, can be mixed with existing soil to form a waterproof lining. However, the product can be expensive and application may be difficult. Check with the natural resource professional on your team to see if this option is appropriate to your location.

**Synthetic Liners:** Synthetic liners are commonly used to create a wetland in smaller more confined schoolyards where there are space limitations or hydrology issues. These wetlands are generally not larger than 2,000 square feet. Materials made of vinyl, polyethylene and butyl rubber are available from various sources such as home improvement stores, water garden suppliers, plumbing supply companies and on the Internet. These materials vary in cost, thickness and width. The most common thickness used on schoolyard habitat projects is 20 or 40 milimeter; the thicker the liner, the heavier and more expensive it will be. Butyl rubber is typically the most expensive, but it is the easiest to handle. Liner materials are manufactured in standard widths; check on the availability of these widths, and size your wetland accordingly. If you need a liner larger than the standard width, you will need to custom order it, adding to the cost. It is important to understand that a liner has to be in one piece, an overlapping seam will not hold water. Also check on the liner's temperature tolerance to make sure it can withstand freezing winters or very hot summers.

**Preform Liners:** Preformed ponds, molded plastic or fiberglass units are commonly used for small water features. This type of liner is not suitable for wildlife use since they have steep slopes and flat bottoms. However, projects using these types of liners can still have curricular benefits.

## Stamp of Approval

It is important to note that in some cases special permission or permits will be needed to complete a project such as wetland restoration, completing earthwork or building structures.
Be sure to contact your state and county government office to find out if any permits are needed.

### Determining Liner Size

Measure the longest and widest points of your wetland. Take the length and add two times the maximum depth, plus three. Do the same thing for the width, and you will have the total length and width you will need for the liner. See the example equation below.

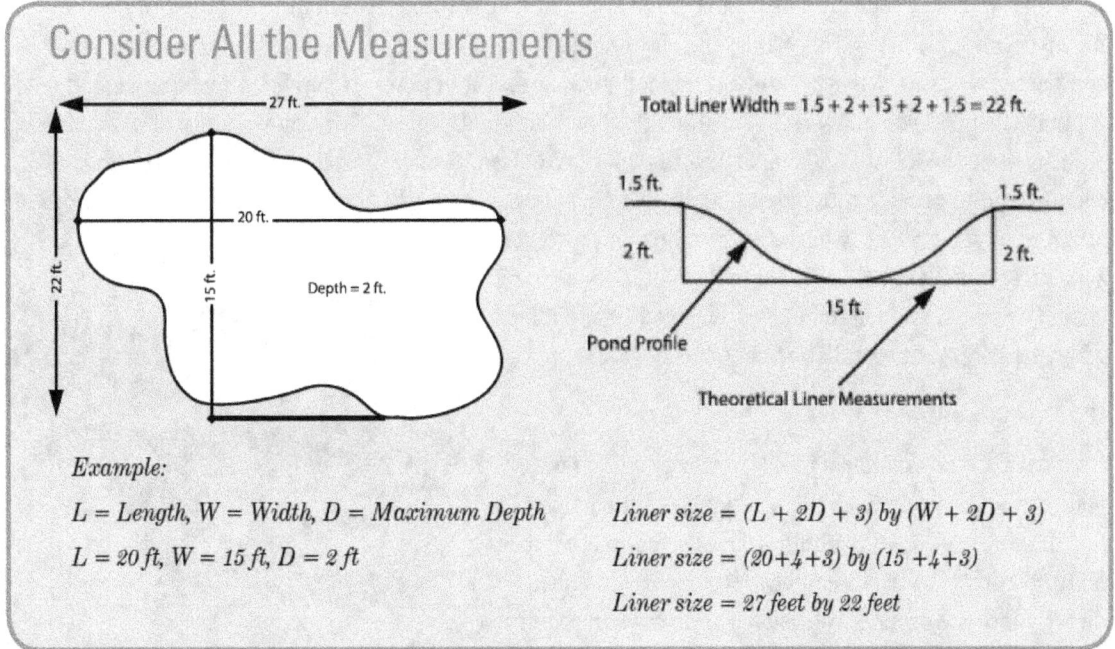

## Consider All the Measurements

27 ft.

20 ft.

22 ft.

15 ft.

Depth = 2 ft.

Total Liner Width = 1.5 + 2 + 15 + 2 + 1.5 = 22 ft.

1.5 ft.

1.5 ft.

2 ft.

2 ft.

15 ft.

Pond Profile

Theoretical Liner Measurements

*Example:*

$L = Length, W = Width, D = Maximum Depth$

$L = 20\,ft, W = 15\,ft, D = 2\,ft$

$Liner\ size = (L + 2D + 3)\ by\ (W + 2D + 3)$

$Liner\ size = (20+4+3)\ by\ (15+4+3)$

$Liner\ size = 27\ feet\ by\ 22\ feet$

## Step 6: Implementation Considerations

### A. Lay Out

Lay out the perimeter of your wetland using something flexible like a garden hose or rope. You may also use spray paint, lime, gypsum, flagging or stakes. Be sure to remind the contractor of any special features of your design, such as an island or the inclusion of existing plants.

### B. Excavate

A professional contractor or experienced volunteer should complete all required excavation. Most projects are completed within one to two days. Before excavation begins, show the contractor where excess soil will be placed. During the excavation phase, make sure all of the edges of the wetland are at the same level and the natural spillway or overflow runs in a desirable direction, away from buildings or other high use areas. If one edge of the wetland is lower, the water

USFWS

*Watching excavation is an exciting experience for students and teachers to see their project being built.*

will overflow on that side. When excavation is complete, return topsoil and sod to the bottom of the wetland to provide roughness and an organic planting medium. Add any planned brush, stumps or other woody debris.

### C. Optional: Install liner.

It is best to install your liner as part of excavation. A delay could result in unfavorable conditions for installation. If using a clay liner, the clay should be applied as uniformly as possible and then compacted. If using a synthetic or preformed liner, secure it in place. If you have rocks or jagged tree roots in the hole, you may need to cushion the liner with materials such as thick layers of newspapers, old carpet or thick layers of sand. Once the liner is in place, return topsoil and sod to the bottom of the wetland to provide roughness and an organic planting medium. Add any planned brush, stumps or other woody debris. Clay liners need to be filled with water soon after completion. If allowed to dry out, the clay may shrink or crack, and fail to hold water. Keep this in mind when creating your installation timeline.

### D. Optional: Build study platform or deck.

Construct a study platform or deck prior to adding water to your wetland. If your deck design requires support posts, install them as soon as possible after excavation is complete. Natural bottom wetlands can have these posts installed directly into the ground. Wetlands with liners will require a concrete stepping stone or deck foundation block, cushioned by the soil, and placed above the liner. Care should be taken to ensure that structures located inside the wetland adhere to safety and ADA regulations.

### E. Plant

Install plants as indicated on your design, adhering to the correct zones and water depths for each plant species. In the event your site receives rainfall to an extent that your planting zones are covered, be prepared to pump out water from your project site, so students do not have to enter the water to install the plants in their proper zones. A gas powered pump is ideal for small sites, while a commercial sized pump may be needed for moving a high volume of water. The contractor who excavates your project may have this equipment. Getting plants to stay in the soil that is under water is difficult, leaving new plants floating.

### F. Fill

Once your plants are planted, start filling your wetland with water, either with forecasted rainfall or municipal water if reasonable. Swimming pool contractors or fire trucks can bring large volumes of water to a site. Water flow from runoff or a hose may cause erosion in fresh soils. Lay a piece of burlap, erosion control fabric or other biodegradable material at the site to alleviate this problem.

## Place Plants with Care

If planting an existing bioretention area, pond or other water catchment basin that has a "cut side" and "fill side," remember that woody plants can only be installed on the "cut side." Roots can cause damage to the "fill side" by growing downward and weakening the berm.

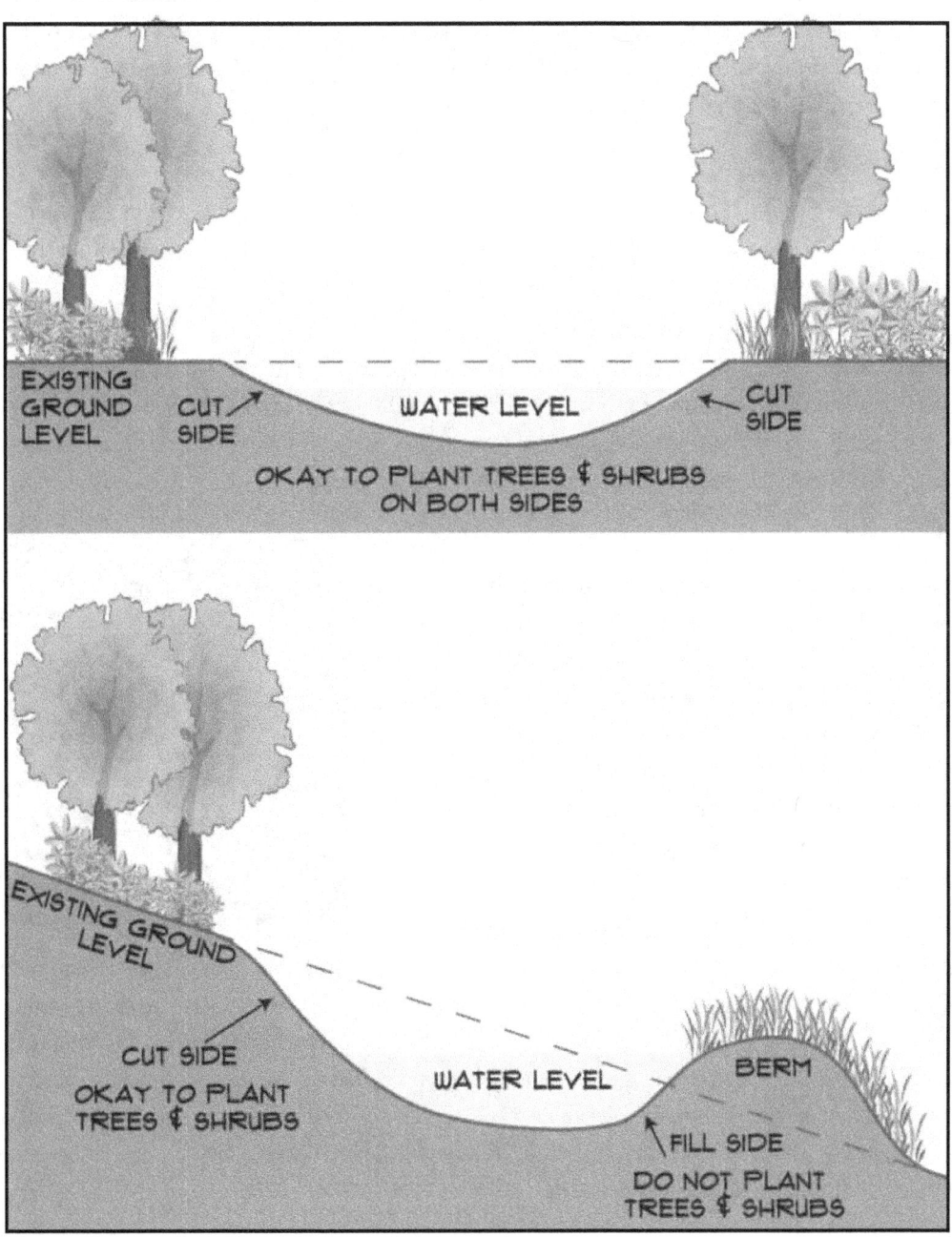

EXISTING GROUND LEVEL    CUT SIDE    WATER LEVEL    CUT SIDE

OKAY TO PLANT TREES & SHRUBS ON BOTH SIDES

EXISTING GROUND LEVEL

CUT SIDE
OKAY TO PLANT TREES & SHRUBS

WATER LEVEL    BERM

FILL SIDE
DO NOT PLANT TREES & SHRUBS

## Step 7: Maintenance Considerations

### Watering

Many wetland plants are adapted to natural fluctuations in water levels. However, if the water floods too deep or too often, or dries out too much, then certain plants may not survive. Therefore, it is important to keep track of water levels and species survival. You should not continually add water to maintain a desired water level. If your wetland does not hold as much water as you planned, you may need to replant different species. Upland plants surrounding your wetland need to be watered as recommended until they become established.

### Adding Wildlife

Being able to observe wildlife is one of the most exciting things about creating wetlands. Be patient. There is no need to add wildlife. Many schoolyard projects become a home to wildlife within the first year. Sometimes it just takes a few weeks or even days.

Unless your wetland is connected to, or close to, a water way, it is unlikely that fish will colonize the space, so adding fish may be reasonable. Consider what types of wildlife you would like to attract before adding fish. Many species of fish will limit the amphibians and aquatic insects that can survive in the wetland. If you do choose to add fish, make sure the species are native to your area. Non-native wildlife species are as harmful to an ecosystem as non-native plants.

### Mosquito Concerns

Frank Marsden

Mosquitoes are part of the natural environment and, as such, can be associated with your habitat. Properly constructed and maintained, your wetland will not be a source of mosquitoes, but will actually help control them. For example, dragonflies and craneflies are frequent early inhabitants of wetlands and their larvae are predators of mosquito larvae. This interaction not only controls your mosquito population, but also provides a great opportunity for student investigations.

There are a few other steps you can take to alleviate common concerns about mosquitoes. If your wetland will hold water year round, you can add native fish. Contact a local fish hatchery to learn which species you should add. Another method to control mosquitoes is the use of a "BTI dunk." Mosquito dunks use the bacterium *Bacilllus thuringiensis* var. *israelensis* that specifically attacks mosquito larvae when applied to standing water. The bacterium will not harm fish or other animals. You can also add an aerator or fountain to your wetland. Mosquitos thrive in standing water. Keeping movement in the water will help deter them. However, these devices usually add additional maintenance concerns.

# Appendix D: Other Project Features

Your project design may call for other human use features. Below are a few sample designs. Talk with your community members to seek out other designs and ideas.

## Sample Bench Design

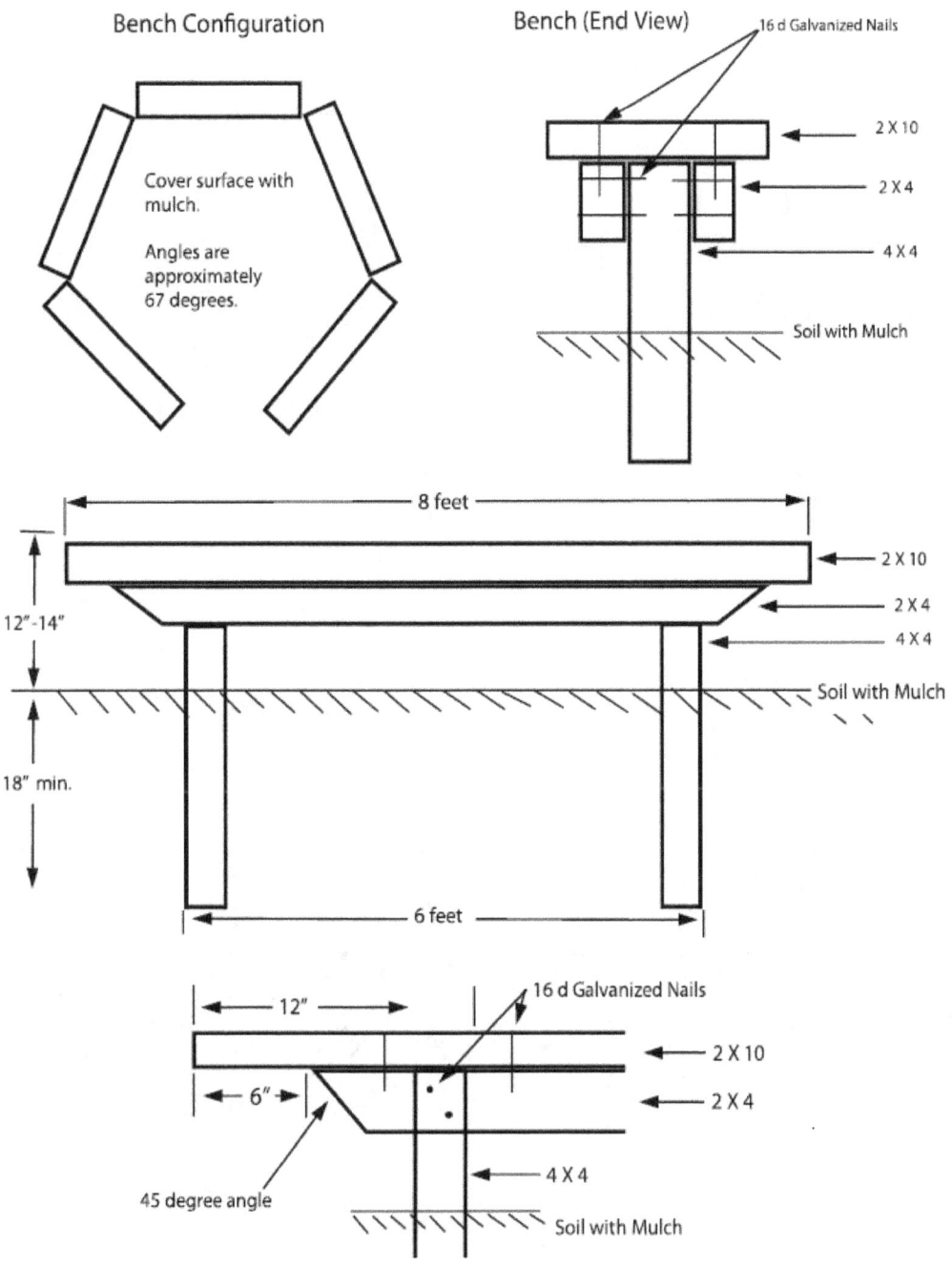

Bench Configuration

Cover surface with mulch.

Angles are approximately 67 degrees.

Bench (End View)

16 d Galvanized Nails

2 X 10

2 X 4

4 X 4

Soil with Mulch

8 feet

2 X 10

2 X 4

4 X 4

Soil with Mulch

12"-14"

18" min.

6 feet

12"

6"

16 d Galvanized Nails

2 X 10

2 X 4

4 X 4

45 degree angle

Soil with Mulch

*Typical outdoor bench design. Note that all lumber is pressure treated yellow pine. Nails are 16 penny galvanized screw or ring shank. Landscape timbers may be substituted for the 4 x 4 material. Nails are spaced 12 inches apart off center. Design by Ronald K. Jones, U.S. Fish and Wildlife Service.*

## Sample Study Platform/Deck Design

FRONT POND VIEW

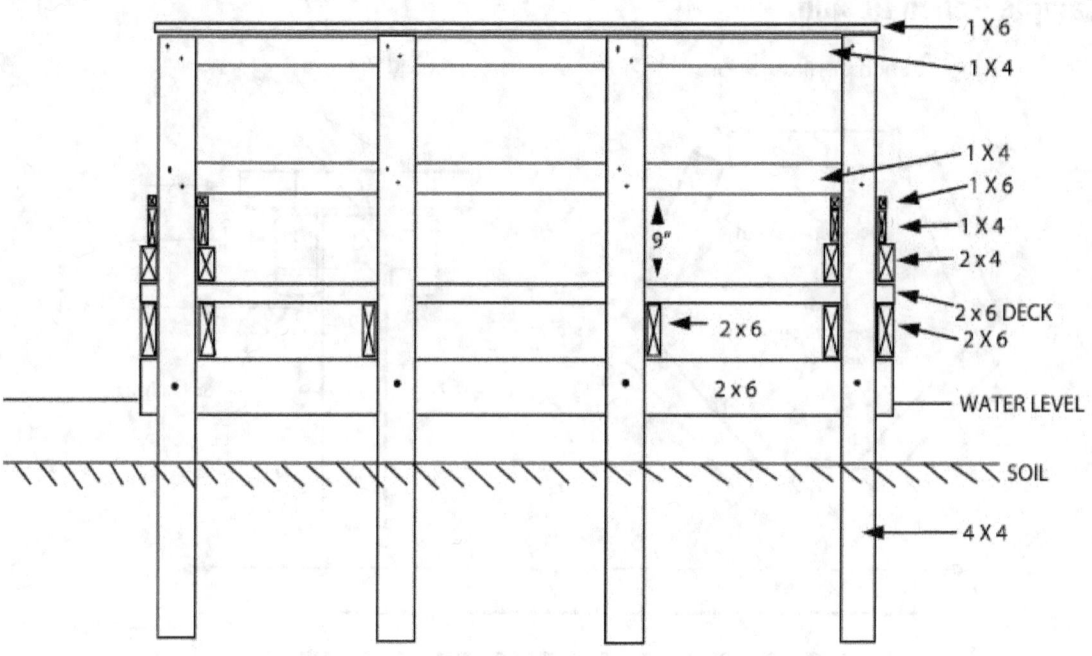

SIDE VIEW

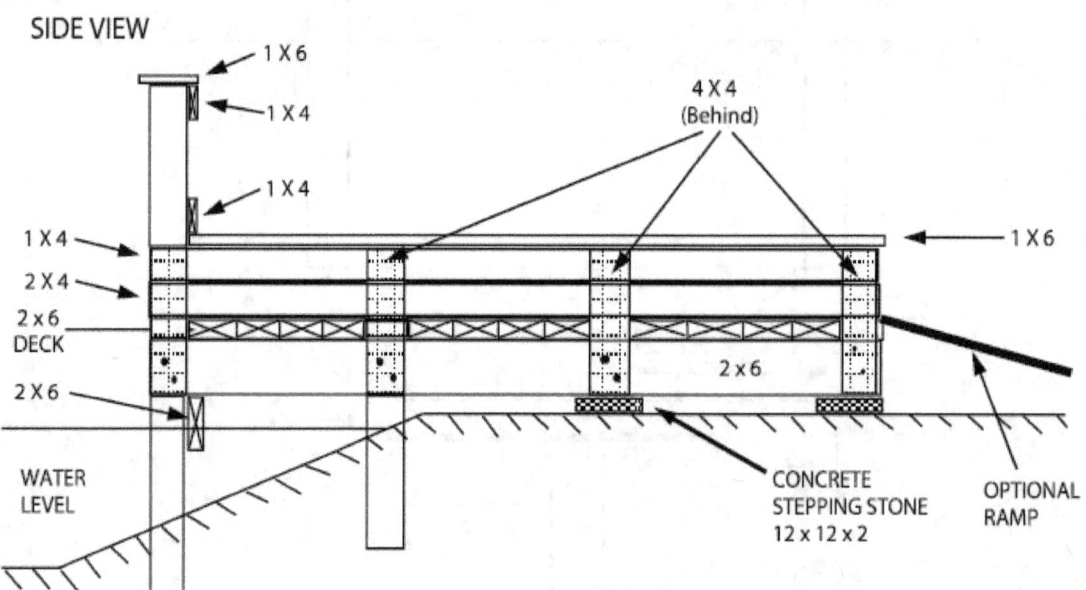

*Style and dimensions of the platform may vary with need, construction techniques, site modifications, etc. Note that all wood is pressure treated. All fasteners are galvanized. Design by Ronald K. Jones, U.S. Fish and Wildlife Service.*

# Appendix E: Commonly Used Equipment

Listed below are common types of equipment used during project installation. Smaller equipment such as a sod cutter or tiller can be rented and used by an adult volunteer, while the larger equipment needs to be operated by a licensed contractor. Work with your local natural resource professional and the contractor to determine the equipment needed.

USFWS
Sod cutter

USFWS
Skid steer loader

USFWS
Backhoe

USFWS
Excavator

USFWS
Bulldozer

USFWS
Brush-hog

**Sod cutter:** A sod cutter is used to remove sod. It is gas powered and operated like a heavy push behind mower. It creates strips of sod that can be rolled up and removed.

**Skid steer loader:** A skid steer loader is commonly referred to as a Bobcat. They are used with a front end bucket in small and hard to reach locations such as between buildings or courtyards. Generally, they are limited to excavation projects that are less than 10,000 square feet. This type of machinery also can be used to remove sod. When doing so, maintain a very shallow cut to reduce soil disturbance.

**Backhoe:** Tractors with a back hoe and front end bucket are suitable for wetland projects that are less than 10,000 square feet.

**Excavator:** Excavators usually have tracks for mobility and come in various sizes and are used on projects larger than 10,000 square feet. They are designed for digging only and not for relocating soil beyond the project boundary. They can be very effective on sites that are too wet for bulldozers.

**Bulldozer:** Bulldozers are the most accessible and provide the best utility and cost effectiveness for this type of work. There are small dozers such as the D-3 and medium size such as the D-4 which are sufficient for wetland projects smaller than 1 acre. When developing an acre or larger wetland, a D-5 or D-6 bulldozer would be the best selection for the project. Bulldozers can construct the wetland and handle the leveling and grooming.

**Brush-hog:** Brush-hogs are not excavation equipment, but are large mowers used for projects that need to clear overgrowth or tall vegetation to create a path or clear a project site for excavation.

# Appendix F: Additional Resources

## Resources for Why to Create a Schoolyard Habitat Project

Civic Results. (2008). *Community Action Guide: Building the Children & Nature Movement From the Ground Up*. Denver, Colorado: Children & Nature Network.

Coffey, Ann. (2004). *Asking Children Listening to Children: School Grounds Transformation*. Ottawa, Ontario, Canada: Canadian Biodiversity Institute.

Louv, Richard. (2006). *Last Child in the Woods*. Chapel Hill, North Carolina: Algonquin Books.

Nabhan, Gary Paul, and Stephen A. Trimble. (1994). *The Geography of Childhood: Why Children Need Wild Places*. Boston, Massachusetts: Beacon Press.

Sobel, David. (1996). *Beyond Ecophobia: Reclaiming the Heart in Nature Education*. Great Barrington, Massachusetts: The Orion Society and the Myrin Institute.

Sobel, David. (2004). *Place-Based Education: Connecting Classrooms and Communities*. Great Barrington, Massachusetts: The Orion Society and the Myrin Institute.

## Resources for How to Create a Schoolyard Habitat Project

Arbor Day Foundation. (2007). *Learning with Nature Idea Book: Creating Nurturing Outdoor Spaces for Children*. Lincoln, Nebraska: The Arbor Day Foundation and Dimensions Educational Research Foundation.

Bucklin-Sporer, Arden, and Rachel Kathleen Pringle. (2010). *How to Grow a School Garden: A Complete Guide for Parents and Teachers*. Portland, Oregon: Timber Press.

Coffey, Ann. (2006). *A Guide to Transforming School Grounds*. Ottawa, Canada: Canadian Biodiversity Institute.

Finstad, Kristina, Christiane Parry, and Eben Schwartz. (2008). *Digging In: A Guide to Community-Based Habitat Restoration*. San Francisco, California: California Coastal Commission.

Grant, Tim, and Gail Littlejohn, editors. (2001). *Greening School Grounds: Creating Habitats for Learning*. Gabriola Island, British Columbia, Canada: New Society Publishers.

Karen L. Ripple, and Edgar W. Garbisch. (2000). *POW! The Planning of Wetlands: An Educator's Guide*. St. Michael's Maryland: Environmental Concern, Inc. http://www.wetland.org

Kays, Jonathan, Joy Drohan, Adam Downing, and Jim Finley. (2006). *Woods in Your Backyard: Learning to Create and Enhance Natural Areas around Your Home*. College Park, Maryland: University of Maryland, Maryland Cooperative Extension.

Moore, Robin C. (1993). *Plants for Play: A Plant Selection Guide for Children's Outdoor Environments*. Berkley, California: Mig Communications.

Tallamy, Douglas W. (2007). *Bringing Nature Home: How You Can Sustain Wildlife with Native Plants*. Portland, Oregon: Timber Press.

## Resources for Use of your Schoolyard Habitat Project

American Forest Foundation. (2010). *Project Learning Tree.* http://www.plt.org/

Broda, Herbert W. (2007). *Schoolyard Enhanced Learning, Using the Outdoors as an Instructional Tool, K-8.* Portland, Maine: Stenhouse Publishers.

Carlson, LaVonne, editor. (2004). *Flying Wild: An Educator's Guide to Celebrating Birds.* Houston, Texas: Council for Environmental Education. http://www.flyingwild.org/

Coffey, Ann. (2004). *School Grounds in a Box: A Guide to Building a Model for Redesigning Your School Grounds.* Ottawa, Ontario, Canada: Canadian Biodiversity Institute.

Cornell, Joseph. (1979). *Sharing Nature with Children.* Nevada City, California: Dawn Publications.

Council for Environmental Education. (2010). *Project WILD.* http://www.projectwild.org/

Earth Partnership for Schools. (2010). *Earth Partnership for Schools Curriculum Guide.* University of Wisconsin, Madison Arboretum. http://uwarboretum.org/eps/

Jaffe, Roberta, and Gary Appel. (1990). *The Growing Classroom: Garden-Based Science.* Reading, Massachusetts: Addison-Wesley Publishers.

Kesselheim, Alan S., Britt E. Slattery, Susan Higgins, and Mark R. Schilling. (2003). *Wow! The Wonders of Wetlands: An Educator's Guide.* St. Michael's Maryland: The Watercourse and Environmental Concern, Inc. http://www.wetland.org

Project Wet Foundation. (2010). *Project Wet: Worldwide Water Education.* http://projectwet.org/

USFWS

# Glossary

**Bioswale:** Landscape elements designed to remove silt and pollution from surface run-off water, similar to a raingarden the main difference being its linear swale shape.

**Canopy:** The top layer in the forest and is made of the tallest trees.

**Decomposed granite:** Also called DG or crushed gravel, small pieces of weathered rock approved for building ADA accessible trails and pathways.

**Erosion:** Describes the transport of solids in the environment by wind or water; it is a natural process but has been increased dramatically by human land-use.

**Growing season:** The period of each year when native plants grow determined by climate and elevation, other environmental factors that affect the growing season include location, temperature, daylight hours and rainfall.

**Hedgerow:** A line of closely spaced shrubs and trees, planted to form a barrier or mark the boundary of an area.

**Herbaceous:** Plants with soft or fleshy stems.

**Infiltration:** The migration of water through soil.

**Integrated Pest Management Plan:** Coordinates economically and environmentally acceptable methods of pest control with the careful and minimal use of toxic pesticides.

**Phenology:** The scientific study of periodic biological phenomena, such as flowering, breeding, and migration, in relation to climatic conditions.

**Raingarden:** A shallow planted depression designed to collect, absorb and clean rainwater run-off from impervious surfaces. A typical raingarden consists of native plants, loose soil, mulch and sometimes gravel.

Frank Marsden

**Restoration:** The process of bringing back to existence, or reestablishing, the original condition of a degraded environment.

**Runoff:** An overflow of rainfall that cannot be absorbed by soil and vegetation.

**Storm-water retention basin:** Sometimes called a wet pond it collects storm-water runoff through a system of street and parking lot drains to prevent flooding and downstream erosion, and improve water quality within the watershed.

**Topography:** Lay of the land, including surface configuration, contours, slopes and drainage patterns.

**Watershed:** The entire land area that contributes surface runoff to a given drainage system.

**Windbreak:** One or more rows of trees or shrubs planted to provide shelter from wind and protect soil from erosion. If designed properly, windbreaks around a building can reduce the cost of heating and cooling and save energy.

**Xeriscaping:** Landscaping and gardening in ways that reduce or eliminate the need for supplemental water from irrigation.